# Escape Velocity

## Better Metrics for Agile Teams

## Doc Norton

# Escape Velocity

## Better Metrics for Agile Teams

Doc Norton

ISBN 978-0-578-64483-7

Leanpub

This is a Leanpub book. Leanpub empowers authors and publishers with the Lean Publishing process. Lean Publishing is the act of publishing an in-progress ebook using lightweight tools and many iterations to get reader feedback, pivot until you have the right book and build traction once you do.

*To My Children and Grandchildren*

*Courtney, Sean,*
*Emerson, Liam,*
*Caleb, and Ethan*

*If there is one thing I wish I'd learned much sooner in life,*
*it is this:*

*You have nothing more precious than your time.*
*Give it to the people you love most.*

# Contents

# About

## This Book

"Escape Velocity" is a record of my own journey as I learn about agile, metrics, and team dynamics. It is a snapshot, a moment in time. The content herein is the result of more than 30 years of learning about and practicing software development. I've a lot to learn. I always will. The more we know about a topic, the more we realize we don't know enough about it. This isn't a prescription or recipe. It's thoughts. My thoughts. I hope they help you.

## The Title

"Escape Velocity" is the minimum speed needed for an object to escape from a massive body[1]. Once an object achieves escape velocity, it is able to free itself from the force of the massive body without any additional impulse.

I thought this non-risque double entendre was fun. Not only are we saying a team can "escape velocity" as a metric. But we are saying there is an "escape velocity" at which point agile teams can escape the massive body of Scrum and learn about the broader universe of agile.

---

[1]Escape velocity. (2017, March 21). Retrieved March 26, 2017, from https://en.wikipedia.org/wiki/Escape_velocity

# The Author

Bumbling and stumbling toward love, light, and good. Hoping to make the world a better place one tiny contribution at a time.

Co-Founder of OnBelay, Doc is passionate about working with teams to improve delivery, helping leaders be more effective, and building great organizations. Once a dedicated code slinger, Doc has turned his energy toward helping teams, departments, and companies work better together in the pursuit of better software. Working with a wide range of companies such

Doc Norton (@DocOnDev)

as Groupon, Nationwide Insurance, and Belly, Doc has applied tenants of agile, lean, systems thinking, and host leadership to develop highly effective cultures and drastically improve their ability to deliver valuable software and products.

# Preface

I've been practicing some form of iterative and incremental software delivery for quite some time. In the early 1990s, I worked with Joseph Sladick on a project where he taught me about incremental delivery as a means of not getting too far before getting feedback. We didn't work in set iterations, but we did work in small chunks.

When I formed my first software studio, I brought these concepts to the team we built. In building software for paying customers, we started a practice of regular status meetings. In doing so, the chunking of the work changed slightly so that we could deliver something every couple of weeks. We'd taken on a practice we called "shadowing" where developers would work together on harder problems or to speed up on-boarding to projects. Here, developers would sit together and work on the same deliverable at the same time.

In November of 1999, I purchased "XP Explained" by Kent Beck and realized I'd found my tribe. These people were doing some crazy stuff with estimating and testing, which I was a bit leery of, but they'd honed a lot of the other things we were playing with; so why not give it a try?

A few years later, I'd sold off the company and found myself in a senior leadership position at a large regional bank that was interested in "this agile thing." An avid XP practitioner, I had a casual relationship with Scrum and Scrum was what they wanted. So I flew to Chicago to get my Scrum Master Certification from Ken Schwaber. Words like Sprint, Points, Chicken and Pig, and Burn-Down and Velocity all became a part of my vernacular.

For the following few years, whether as an employee or consultant, I was spreading the Scrum way. I like to believe I did well; that

I made a positive difference. The teams I worked with improved. They got better at quality. They got better at delivering solutions that delighted customers. They got better at working together. But they rarely got better at estimating or forecasting with velocity.

Thanks to a crafty certification scheme, Scrum grew very popular in the corporate world. You could send people to two days of training and get them certified.

Boom!
You're agile.
Easy peasy.

Over time, I started to see more teams myopically focused on their velocity. Teams engaged in all sorts of behavior in attempts to make their velocity look like they thought it was supposed to. Managers set velocity goals and pushed teams to move faster.

So, I eventually wrote a talk about how velocity isn't supposed to be a goal. In the research for that talk, I came across a number of new ideas and interesting perspectives on measurements, metrics, and behaviors. Feedback from audiences who've heard that talk, along with several more years of practice eventually led me to this book.

I hope you find it useful. I am not anti-Scrum. I think it is far too often implemented improperly and has become twisted over the years. I believe this to be a result of Scrum's light-weight certification diluting the pool of "experienced" practitioners.

I'd say I am anti-velocity at this point. It is a poor metric that offers far less value than the angst that results from the perpetual misuse.

Hopefully, you find value herein and come away with a better set of tools for helping teams forecast and get to predictability.

 Velocity is a poor metric that offers far less value than the angst that results from the perpetual misuse.

# What is Velocity?

## Velocity is a Vector

A vector is an entity that has both magnitude (size) and direction. Velocity indicates the speed of something in a particular direction.

In physics, velocity is the rate at which an object changes its position [2]. An object that oscillates at a high speed, but always returns to its starting position has a zero velocity.

Velocity is the rate at which a team delivers value to the customer. A team that completes many tasks, but delivers no value to the customer should have a zero velocity.

In agile software development, velocity is the rate at which a team delivers value to the customer. Value is quantifiable, and we can therefore say it has size. The direction is indicated by the traversal from idea to implementation. A team that completes many tasks, but delivers no value to the customer should have a zero velocity.

I say "should" because I see an awful lot of teams that measure velocity based on criteria other than value to the customer. Some consider a story done when development is complete. Others are a tad more "mature" and count a story as done when it is ready to go to production. Not actually in production, mind you; that takes weeks - what with manual testing requirements and change control procedures and getting into queue for the operations team... And some teams consider a story complete once it is actually in

[2]Speed and Velocity. (n.d.). Retrieved March 18, 2017, from http://www.physicsclassroom.com/class/1DKin/Lesson-1/Speed-and-Velocity

production. But even that *assumes* value to the customer. What if you didn't count a story as done until customers were actually using it and liked it? If velocity is the rate at which we deliver value to the customer, wouldn't a true measure of velocity include verification of value delivery?

But I digress a bit, perhaps.

For the sake of this book, let's go with "in production" means done. In this book, we won't get into details of how to deliver at the end of each iteration, much less continuous delivery. Instead of technical techniques, we'll focus on what to measure, how to measure, why to measure it, and how to use the measurements for good rather than evil.

# Velocity is a Lagging Indicator

Velocity is also a lagging indicator. It is a measurement taken at the end of a series of steps. We plan, we prioritize, we work, we test, and then we measure.

## Lagging Indicators are Abstract

Lagging indicators tend to be aggregate or abstract. They don't provide detailed insight into the operations, rather they provide an indication of results. Net profit is a lagging indicator for a company. While it tells us about how the company is doing, it gives us no indication of why the organization was or was not successful.

Let's look at another lagging indicator; unemployment. The unemployment index is a lagging indicator. It tells us whether or not unemployment is on the rise or decline, which in turns tells us if the economy is doing poorly or well, respectively. An increase in unemployment means a sagging economy. A decrease in unemployment means a growing economy. But there is nothing about unemployment that tells us why the economy is performing in a particular manner or how we might go about making an adjustment to economic policy to bolster growth. Moreover, the way to bolster the economy is not to focus on unemployment, but to address the underlying issues.

Historically, policies focused on training and jobs creation have had little or even negative impact on employment among the populations the programs target [3]. Those that did create new jobs, such as the Works Progress Administration of the 1930s and the Public Employment Program of the 1970s and 1980s, did little to impact generation of jobs outside of those directly created and funded by the programs. Essentially, these created an artificial drop in unemployment, but did not address underlying causes. Each program resulted in a corresponding increase in unemployment once government funding ran out.

Conversely, policies focused on addressing broader monetary and fiscal trends can result in a boost in Aggregate Demand, which then leads to a decrease in unemployment.

Similarly, one of the problems with velocity as a lagging indicator is that while it can tell how much work we delivered over a given time period, it cannot tell how well the team is doing at ensuring consistent delivery or at improving their process overall. Velocity provides little to no insight into root causes of process issues.

Moreover, attempts to increase velocity directly tend to either create artificial increases that are not sustainable, or result in other more detrimental issues, whereas efforts to address underlying causes more often than not result in improvements in velocity. Managing story composition and limiting work in process results in smoother flow, which leads to a more stable velocity and the ability for a team to mature into more rapid delivery.

---

[3]Contributor, D. M. (2017, March 14). So far, federal job-training programs have been outright failures. Retrieved April 27, 2017, from http://thehill.com/blogs/pundits-blog/economy-budget/323885-thus-far-federal-job-training-programs-have-been-an

A stable or slightly increasing velocity is usually considered a good thing. When managers see a stable velocity from iteration to iteration, they may become complacent and forgo any improvement efforts. But the reality is that there are actually numerous factors that impact a team's ability to deliver and the current velocity trend may be more a matter of coincidence than performance. We will look at a number of factors that impact velocity in later sections.

## Lagging Indicators are Poor Short-term Predictors

Lagging indicators[4] tend to be weak indicators for the short-term and are much more reliable for confirming long-term trends.

Let's take a look at "velocity" in a different industry.

For retail, we can use sales volume as our "velocity". Sales volume is a lagging indicator which tells us something about how we did in the prior period, but does not give us any indication as to why sales were high or low.

The following graph shows 10 years of retail sales for a narrow set of products. From this graph, we can discern some patterns. We know Q4 sales are consistently higher than the others. And we know that Q1 sales are normally the lowest at approximately 75% of the prior Q4. We can also see that the sales from the prior quarter is often not a good indicator of what the next quarter's sales will be. Sure, we can look at the long history and determine average percentages and apply that to get a fairly good guess. But we need the long history. Looking at only the prior quarter's sales is insufficient for determining the next quarter's sales.

---

[4]Leading vs. Lagging KPIs â€" What Successful Companies Measure. (2016, August 17). Retrieved March 18, 2017, from https://www.accountexnetwork.com/blog/2014/10/leading-indicators/

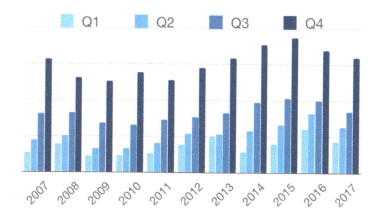

Retail Sales Volume by Period

Similarly, our velocity from the immediately concluded iteration is not often a good indicator of what the velocity will be in the next iteration. From one iteration to the next, velocity can vary wildly due to any number of factors.

Like retail sales, despite the short-term volatility, we can look at velocity over time and confirm trends we might suspect, such as a lower average velocity during holiday seasons. This doesn't tell us what the velocity will be in November or December, but it does let us know that the odds are good these months will have lower velocity numbers than September or October.

# Velocity as a Measure of a Complex System

This is ultimately quite significant. Velocity, while a simple concept, is actually a measure of output for a complex system. Think about the number of factors that go into a velocity measurement. There is the organizational mission, the broader business objectives, and the objective of the product itself. There are product owners, designers, architects, developers, testers, subject matter experts, security specialists, database specialists, governance, and production specialists involved. There are stand-ups, planning meetings, and retrospectives. There are epics, stories, and tasks all tracked on a board or in a system with multiple lanes representing different key states in the delivery of each single piece of work. After all these individuals interact with one another, responding to change, and collaborating with the customer in pursuit of working software, we take a single measurement. That single measurement represents the interactions of the individuals and all of their adaptions to change in the delivery of working software.

Velocity is a simple measure of a very complex system.

 To measure creative work by throughput alone is to not measure it at all; quality and impact are essential.

While a simple measure of a complex system may sound ideal, in this case, it is generally insufficient. Velocity doesn't tell us enough to be particularly useful. From velocity alone one cannot ferret out root causes. One cannot determine conclusively that the team is doing better (or worse) from a rising (or falling) velocity.

Velocity is but one dimension to consider. To measure creative work by throughput alone is to not measure it at all; quality and impact are essential.

## Velocity By Way of Analogy

Knowing that velocity is a lagging indicator of a complex system is interesting, but what does it really indicate? Perhaps an analogy can help us out here - There is something we all have in common that is also a lagging indicator of a complex system - our body weight.

Our body weight is a lagging indicator of a complex system. There are inputs and outputs and there are multiple factors that impact the system overall. From our diet and exercise to genetics and even our social network, there are numerous factors that impact our body weight. As we've covered, the same is true for a team's velocity. Multiple factors impact a team's velocity.

By body weight alone, can we tell if an individual is healthy?

If I were to tell you our patient's name is "Pat" and their body weight is 130, could you tell me definitively if Pat were in good or poor health? What about a body weight of 100? What about a body weight of 300? If Pat is a linebacker for the Detroit Lions, 300 pounds might be a perfectly healthy body weight. So the answer is, no. Body weight alone cannot reliably tell you if the individual is healthy.

Moreover, if the body weight were in a range that strongly suggested poor health, say 600 pounds, you could not ascertain from the body weight alone what to do for this individual to help them shed weight in a healthy manner.

The same is true of velocity. Knowing a team's velocity cannot reliably tell you if the team is "healthy". Adding to the challenge is the fact that velocity has no baseline standard. There is no commonly accepted range within which velocity falls, so our assessment of health gets even more difficult. It is common to see a team with a consistent velocity of 100 or more points per iteration being outperformed by a team with a consistent velocity of 30 points. Points don't translate from team to team, save basic trending. In general, more points is more software delivered and fewer points is less software delivered. This is assuming, of course, that you don't point tasks and other non-creation work. If you do that, you'll likely see little to no correlation between velocity and delivery of software.

 Knowing a team's velocity cannot reliably tell you if the team is "healthy".

Now we do know that a velocity of 0 is generally an indication of poor health. And just like with bodyweight, while we know the patient is in poor health, we don't have enough data to make an informed recommendation for improvement. We can say generic things like, "Go on a diet", or, "Focus on getting to done", but we cannot provide specific targeted advice with the information we have.

We've shown that the measure itself is not necessarily an indication of health. And we've further shown that even when we can ascertain poor health, the measure does not tell us enough to diagnose the actual problem. As a result, we cannot make a solid recommendation for how to get to good health.

Now, let's continue with this analogy just a bit more.

Let's say that you wake up one morning and you decide that you want to lose 15 pounds. You used to weigh less and you're tired of the number you see on the scale.

Take a moment and think about all the ways you might go about losing 15 pounds.

Perhaps you would increase your daily step count or take up jogging. Maybe you'd cut back on carbohydrates or you'd increase your intake of salad. You could reduce portion sizes or stop snacking at 7pm each night. Cut back on sugars, replace soda with water, take up crossfit, train for a marathon, or stand while you work. There are any number of things you could do that would likely improve your health and reduce the weight.

But if you're strictly focused on the weight; if you're not measuring any other aspect of your health such as cholesterol, sugar levels, or cardiovascular endurance, you might make other decisions to ensure you get to the goal body weight. You could starve yourself. You could consume nothing but water for 30 days. You could smoke crack. You could sever a limb.

Sure, some of these seem ridiculous, but that is precisely the point.

Let's say we are using only one measurement of health. And that one measurement doesn't tell us enough about the system that produced it. If this is the case, then we can't really determine what behavior improves the overall health of the system nor can we tell which behavior harms the overall system. In general, the less we understand about a system, the more we are likely to engage in behavior that harms the overall system and the less we are likely to engage in behavior that helps it.

 Without sufficient data about the system we can neither properly diagnose our ills nor make informed remediation decisions.

Even our "healthy" options for losing 15 pounds are subjective. For some, training for a marathon would be riskier than making no lifestyle change. I suspect many of you feel you fall into that category.

Without sufficient data about the system we can neither properly diagnose our ills nor make informed remediation decisions.

Just as our bodyweight doesn't tell us enough about our system to inform our lifestyle choices, velocity doesn't tell us enough about our system to inform our process choices.

# Velocity Anti-Patterns

If you've been on an agile team that uses velocity as a key metric, you've probably experienced, or at least witnessed, some pretty strange behavior.

I asked a group of agile coaches and practitioners via Twitter and LinkedIn about dysfunctions they've seen on teams related to the use of velocity. I received plenty of responses that inspired head shaking and hand wringing. I pulled out the most commonly identified issues related to velocity and metrics, and share them here.

This is by no means comprehensive, but it is a reasonable representation of the issues that exist within organizations when it comes to metrics and management.

## Before We Get Started

I want to be crystal clear here: The Velocity Anti-Patterns listed here are not necessarily indications of measuring and reporting velocity. Many are indications of the pervasiveness of poor management.

 Velocity is a tool and nothing more. It is not until the human element is introduced that the tool becomes potentially dangerous.

You see, velocity itself is not necessarily harmful. It is a tool and nothing more. Just as a knife is a tool and nothing more. It is not until the human element is introduced that the tool becomes potentially dangerous. Whether deliberate or inadvertent, it is interaction with the tool that introduces risk. The better fit the tool is for purpose and the more deliberate and informed the individual, the lower the risk.

So with that in mind, let's take a look at some of the most common Velocity Anti-Patterns identified by the coaches and practitioners.

# Demand for Higher Velocity

This is far and away, the most common Velocity Anti-Pattern, and quite possibly the most harmful. It manifests itself in a number of differing fashions, but the basics are the same: Somebody determines that the team needs to get more done in less time. So they send out the message - "We are going to need more velocities." This person is usually an authority figure and typically doesn't do the actual work being asked of the team. And they clearly don't know what velocity is. More velocities? Aw, C'mon, really?

## Why We Need "More Velocities"

In some cases, the need for higher velocity is based on a set scope for a set date and some basic math - with significantly flawed assumptions. Take the total work to be done and divide it by the team's average velocity. If the number of weeks to complete the work exceed the number of weeks between now and the deadline, then the team needs to get more done in less time. All of this typically under-represents the volatility of the velocity, fails to take into account systemic issues, is based on estimates made with very little information, and assumes a known and locked scope.

In other cases, a potential for higher velocity is observed, which then creates a demand for higher velocity. These observations are steeped in a lack of true understanding of creative work and an adherence to a Tayloristic[5] output-centric management style. The team can be seen "loafing". There are times where nobody is actively writing code. There are times where more than one individual is working on the same basic piece of work at a given time. Sometimes, we can even see two or more people working at the same computer at the same time. Not everybody punches in at 8am and out again at 6pm. Some people don't eat lunch at their desks. And who knows what people are actually doing when they "work from home"? With such an output-centric perspective, one might assume that this team can clearly move faster - we just need to give them a little push.

And in other cases, the need for higher velocity is borne of expectation. Everybody knows that when a team goes agile, they get faster. It's a fact. It has been written in numerous agile books, especially books on scrum. I mean, I just wrote it in this book. So it must be true. And if it is true that teams get faster, all we need to do is help them get there.

These are but a few of any number of reasons why we might expect or "need" the team to move faster. This thinking is, unsurprisingly, flawed. Velocity is not about measuring the team. It is about having a coarse-grained forecast. Rather than a tool to rate and push a team, it is a tool to help make key business decisions. Which features can we cut back on? What is truly priority? How else might we organize the work, support the team, or think about the product?

 Velocity isn't about measuring the team. It is about having a coarse-grained forecast.

Unfortunately, these are hard decisions. They may force us to make tradeoffs. They may result in our having to change our public message; to move a date or to reset market expectations. It is far

[5]What is Taylorism? Retrieved April 12, 2017, - http://www.businessdictionary.com/definition/Taylorism.html

easier to defer the hard decision and ask a team to "step up". It is easier to abdicate the responsibility and push it to the team.

In most cases where the need for an increase in velocity is articulated, there is an underlying unspoken premise. The belief that if properly motivated, we can do better. Re-phrased, the belief that we are not already operating at our best.

**Given** we need to hit a deadline with a set scope
**When** the team is not moving fast enough to hit the deadline
**Then** the team is capable of moving faster

This is logically flawed. The conclusion is baseless and is in no way supported by the precedents. Just because we *want* a team to move faster does not mean that they can. And quite often, pushing a team to go faster ultimately slows them down.

## Attempts to Entice More Velocities

Leaders (and teams) attempt to achieve velocity increases in numerous ways. Most, as you can imagine, have unintended side effects on the teams and none significantly improve the actual flow/delivery of value to their customers. Here we explore a few ways teams might be encouraged to increase their velocity. Unfortunately, no matter how well intentioned, using such techniques still has a negative impact.

### Increase Awareness

The number one motivational technique is simply to increase awareness. We make the team acutely aware of the deadline, the desired scope, and how near or far they are to hitting the target. This is a simple and passive technique. The idea here is that if people know what is required, they will rise to the occasion.

Burn down charts and burn up charts are a common technique for showing the team how they are doing within an iteration or towards a release. No one can be accused of pressuring a team by simply making data available, right?

But no matter how seemingly benign, this approach invokes the Hawthorne Effect, which practically guarantees the measurement will improve, but does not guarantee the overall results will improve.

I am not saying that you should not use charts or make data available to the team. What I am saying is that you need to be aware that the team will tend toward behavior that "improves" the measurements by which they feel they are being evaluated.

More often than not, velocity will appear to increase. This is often the result of some increase in the average estimate of a story, resulting in higher velocity numbers but no measurable increase in value. The team begins to wonder if they're estimating correctly. Maybe that 3 is really a 5; we're not entirely positive how complex it is. Better to be safe than sorry. We don't want an artificially low velocity - you know, like we used to have.

Measurements should be data the team considers valuable and wishes to see rather than data that management wants for evaluation or demands for process consistency. If management is going to mandate certain measurements, educate the team on what the measurements are and how they serve the team and the organization. Finally - if management is going to mandate certain measurements, then make sure the mandated measurements are well balanced and genuinely serve the team.

## Velocity Goals

So we've shown the team how they are doing. We gave them the burn charts and they still didn't go fast enough. What is a good ScrumMaster to do? Well, help them with the math, of course.

"Hey team. We can see that our burn chart is looking less than ideal. If we want to hit our deadline - and we *do* want to hit our deadline - it looks like we're going to need to increase our average velocity from 22 to 26 as soon as you can. Whaddya say? Can we count on you to work smarter, not harder?"

This, of course, isn't the only way targets are set. Some managers take a more dictatorial approach.

"Okay team. I didn't want to have to do this, but you people can't seem to figure it out on your own. So much for 'self organizing'. Your velocity sucks. I've looked at your burn chart and you can't possibly make it. Effective immediately, velocity must increase to 26 points. I don't want to hear any whining. You've been lallygagging long enough. Now get back to work."

The language is different, but the intent is the same and the end result is likely the same. Velocity will very likely go up. And again, this does not mean the end result will improve.

In fact, what happens is that we've now invoked Goodhart's Law. In setting a target for a lagging indicator in an attempt to control the system, what has actually happened is we've changed the system, thereby changing what the indicator means. As a result, the measurement is no longer the same as the measurement we were using before and the target doesn't mean what the manager thinks it means.

## Rewards

Rewards for increased velocity fall into a category of their own. Here, we must have some level of awareness. After all, we can't assess an increase in velocity if we have no measure. And we additionally have a target. If we're offering a reward for an increase in velocity, there must be a target or even set of targets to which awards are tied. So we've invoked both Hawthorne Effect and Goodhart's Law.

As we know from prior discussion, this means both that the velocity will increase artificially (or temporarily) and that the velocity measurement will not mean what it once did. But it gets worse.

You see, in knowledge work, financial rewards actually impede performance. That's right. Financial incentives impede performance.

 In knowledge work, financial rewards actually impede performance.

In 1971, Mark Lepper and colleagues at Stanford ran a study wherein they invited students to work on puzzles and games[6]. After a period of time, they started to reward students for their performance. There was a pronounced improvement in performance among some of the students. Then, the rewards were taken away and the students who had shown improvement regressed to levels below their original capability. Some of them stopped participating altogether.

At first glance, one might conclude that the incentives improved individual performance and the problem was not their use, but the fact that they were discontinued. But this is not the case. You see, while some people's performance went up temporarily, the overall performance of the group sagged when incentives were introduced and only worsened when they were then retracted. Extrinsic reward structures for work which people found intrinsically motivating made performance worse.

Numerous other studies[7], including those spearheaded by University of Rochester psychologists Edward Deci and Richard Ryan[8]

[6]Lepper, Greene, Nisbett on the "Overjustification" Hypothesis Retrieved April 15, 2017, - http://courses.umass.edu/psyc360/lepper%20greene%20nisbett.pdf

[7]The influence of strength of drive on functional fixedness and perceptual recognition. Journal of Experimental Psychology, Vol 63(1), Jan 1962, 36-41. Retrieved April 15, 2017, from http://dx.doi.org/10.1037/h0044683

[8]Self-determination theory. (2017, April 07). Retrieved April 15, 2017, from https://en.wikipedia.org/wiki/Self-determination_theory

have shown that rewards often undermine our intrinsic motivation to work on interesting, challenging tasks - especially when they are announced in advance or delivered in a controlling manner.

 Rewards often undermine our intrinsic motivation to work on interesting, challenging tasks

For those select few who actually display an increase in performance on cognitive tasks when offered extrinsic rewards, the reward levels tend to lose impact over time. Whatever incentives are offered eventually become the "new normal" and maintenance of existing performance levels will require increases in reward. This is not a sustainable model.

### Velocity Shaming

While really just a variant on rewards, Velocity Shaming gets a special subsection all to itself as it reveals a more serious leadership shortcoming.

The term reward suggests some form of positive reinforcement. With velocity shaming, we forego the positive reinforcement and instead shame or cavil[9] the team for failure to meet expectations. If the caviler is a seagull manager who swoops in occasionally and craps on the team, then shaming will occur perhaps a few times per quarter and will be about failing to average sufficient velocity. If, on the other hand, the caviler is a micro-manager, the shame-fest will probably occur several times within a single iteration for failure to track to a velocity goal.

The more they pay attention, the shorter the shame cycle. The shorter the shame cycle, the more harm done.

---

[9]To raise irritating and trivial objections; find fault with unnecessarily - Cavil. (n.d.). Retrieved March 19, 2018, from http://www.dictionary.com/browse/caviler

There is holding a team accountable and there is just plain bad leadership. For most teams, the inability to move quickly is systemic. From cross team dependencies and arduous process to insufficient support, staffing, and funding, teams are often burdened with herculean tasks that their leadership could make easier. Shaming a team for their inability to function to your liking in a system which you as management support through inaction is a special kind of awful.

If you are in charge of a team and you do this; and you know who you are. Stop it.

Stop it now.

## Attempts to Show More Velocities

When leadership asks for an increase in velocity, there are a few common behaviors that occur. Each of them are an attempt to satisfy the potentially unrealistic ask.

It is intriguing to me how often a manager will make a change such as this to a system of work and then later proclaim that the team is gaming the system. This is simply not the case. In fact, the gaming of the system is the improper application of targets or goals for lagging indicators. The rest is just natural consequence.

 Managers game the system by setting goals for measures. The rest is natural consequence.

The following are but a few examples of what happens when a manager games the system.

### Inflating Points

A few years back, I was working with an organization where teams were achieving the expected increase in velocity, but leadership didn't feel like things were moving any faster. Selecting one team, we looked at their history and found that their velocity had gone from an average of about 20 points to an average of about 40. On a hunch, we ran a report to figure out the average story size for each iteration. Sure enough, the average story size had gone from around 1.4 to around 3.1. In fact, you could see a punctuated increase in average size followed by a slow but steady incline. The punctuated increase came right around the time leadership introduced the new burn up charts and put a focus on velocity.

Looking at the average number of stories completed per iteration, the numbers were telling. With an average velocity of 20 at 1.4 points per story, they were completing around 14 stories per iteration. With an average velocity of 40 at 3.1 points per story, they were completing around 13 stories per iteration.

Were they in fact moving faster and the stories were coincidentally larger? How could we know for sure?

We took an evenly distributed sampling of stories across the history of the project and printed them out without any sizing information. We then asked the team to size the stories using the same techniques they'd always used. The average story size came out to be approximately 2.8 with earlier stories growing from an average of 1.4 to 2.6.

Had they been gaming the system? No. As we've already discussed; we game the system when we change it, the resulting behaviors are just natural consequence. We can't know for sure if there was, at one time, a deliberate increase in story sizes, but we can say that under the given conditions, the team genuinely believed the larger numbers were more accurate.

## Splitting Points

Splitting points refers to two possible activities; taking partial credit for work picked up in a given iteration - but not completed, or breaking stories up into smaller pieces that add up to more than the original.

## Taking Partial Credit

This isn't really a way of making our velocity look greater, but it is a way of making our velocity look "better", so I've added it here.

Say we have an 8 point story that we pick up mid-iteration and don't complete. At the end of the iteration, we award ourselves 3 points and roll 5 points into the next iteration. The intent, I believe, is to be able to represent the effort expended in each iteration. This allows for a smoother looking burn-down chart across a release. And that means fewer people are asking questions.

Of course, if we're not actually delivering value in a given iteration, we probably shouldn't be taking partial credit based on "effort". And if this is happening consistently, maybe those people should be asking questions.

It is not uncommon for teams that engage in this practice to do it repeatedly. I've seen plenty of teams that split and roll. At the end of an iteration, they split all stories in process and roll the remainders into the next iteration. In some cases, such as when they use an electronic tracking system, they actually create a duplicate card, split the points, and move the new card into the next iteration.

I've also seen this happen across multiple iterations. An 8 point card gets split into 3 done and 5 remaining. That 5 gets split into 2 done and 3 remaining which gets split into 2 and 1. Four iterations to complete an 8 point story. And we've lost all visibility of the lead time and cycle times on that story.

Burn charts look good. Velocity seems pretty consistent. Bonuses will be paid to the ScrumMasters. And yet, we've no idea when the work in this iteration will actually be done. We're foolish enough to proclaim that we consistently get 12 points done per iteration, so this 5 point story should easily get done next iteration. We're ignoring the fact that the work completed in a given iteration was actually started in prior iterations and that odds are very low we'll ever finish 5 points on a card in a single iteration.

## Breaking Up Stories

This one is interesting because it is often done for the wrong reasons, but sometimes it works.

Some teams will take a large story and break it into smaller pieces in order to make it look bigger. Take a team that estimates on a Fibonacci scale where stories are sized as 0, 1, 2, 3, 5, 8, 13, 21, and so on. A 5 point story gets broken into three pieces, each estimated at 2 points. Viola, 5 points becomes 6. Nice. They couldn't convince management it was an 8 (thanks Fibonacci), but through some slight of hand, they bumped it to 6. More Velocities, here we come.

Seems a tad dubious, does it not?

But it can actually work. And I don't mean it can work because it artificially increases your velocity, which it does. I mean it can work because you get more work done in less time.

Assume that stories are split along reasonable seams into chunks of work that can be individually delivered. Now the team has increased the likelihood they can both deliver value in this iteration and improve their throughput.

In some environments I've coached, we've seen an interesting outcome when stories get broken down into smaller slices. We found that when we broke large stories into discrete parts, the average time to deliver all discrete parts was less than the time to deliver the larger story. This held true even when the parts added up to more than the story. We will discuss this further in the section on correlations where we discuss Lead Time by Story Size.

If you're going to split stories, do it for the right reasons. Do it because you want to optimize for learning as you go. Do it because you want improved forecasting. Do it because you want a more consistent delivery cadence. Do it because you want to get working software into the hands of your customers as soon as possible.

And a side effect will be that your actual throughput goes up.

# Cross-team Velocity Comparisons

A common anti-pattern in a great deal of organizations is velocity comparison across teams.

It usually goes something like this:

"Your velocity is 20 and theirs is 50. What are you doing wrong?", asks a manager with good but misguided intentions.

"You cannot compare velocity across teams.", says the agile coach, "Velocity measures are unique to each team."

"Surely, there will be some variance from team to team", the manager agrees, "but a 2x difference must indicate trouble."

Of course, we rarely assume the team reporting a velocity of 50 is the team in trouble. More velocities are always better, right?

Let's dive into this one a bit. Why is it that comparison of velocity across teams is deemed an anti-pattern? Are there situations where comparing velocity across teams is ok?

The short answer is, "No", and here's why.

There is a great deal of debate over how velocity is best calculated. From story points to ideal days to hours. From effort to complexity to duration to value. From comparative to scalar to absolute. From t-shirt sizes to fibonacci to linear. Even when two teams in an organization agree on all of these factors, calibration is still extremely difficult. We're using metaphors to represent guesses about work items for which we've a varying level of shared understanding and varying tolerances for risk.

Imagine this scenario; there are two expedition teams given the same basic challenge. Each is going to embark on a unique hike. The hikes are similar, but not identical.

The boss sets the stage by laying out the overall plan:

"You are about to embark on a multi-day hike over territory none of you has ever before covered in hopes of getting excellent photography. It will be similar to other journeys you've taken, but subtly different in an indeterminate number of ways. Your map is incomplete in parts and the path we've identified is our best guess. We've broken the hike into trail sections based on spots along the way that we think will make great photo opportunities. The terrain will vary significantly; some of it may be new to all but one or two of you. Some of it may be dissimilar to terrain any of you have ever seen."

"With these factors in mind, please indicate the number of units involved in the journey where a unit is a measure of energy expended in completing a section of the trail. Please indicate units on a fibonacci scale with no unit greater than 21."

Each team estimates based on these criteria and then hikes for an hour. At the end of the hour, each team measures the number of units completed. The theory is that they can use this data to better estimate how long it will take them to complete the entire journey. As it works out, Team A completes 20 units in the first hour and Team B completes 45 units in the first hour.

So here is the question - Which team is the better performer?

The truth is, we cannot know that from the data provided. The teams may be similar, but they are not the same. The paths may be similar, but they are not the same. The skills and familiarity of the individuals may be similar, but they are not the same. The detail of the maps may be similar, but they are not the same. The navigability of the paths may be similar, but they are not the same.

In addition, the subjective assessment of anticipated energy expended that each team agrees on will vary not only from team to team, but from session to session on the same team. There are many variables. Velocity (units per hour) is a coarse-grained estimate unique to each team.

Hopefully, we can see that comparing such velocity across teams is an exercise in frustration.

Now returning to software, the analogy holds fairly well. The teams may be similar, but they are not the same. The backlogs may be similar, but they are not the same. The skills and familiarity of the individuals may be similar, but they are not the same. The detail of the stories may be similar, but they are not the same. The product roadmaps may be similar, but they are not the same.

In addition, the subjective assessment of complexity that each team agrees on will vary not only from team to team, but from session to session on the same team. There are many variables. Velocity (points per iteration) is a coarse-grained estimate unique to each team.

# Estimation Teams

One common "solution" to the "problem" described in the section on comparing velocity is to have a core set of individuals do all of the estimates. The thinking being that consistency in the estimation makes delivery comparable. While I have seen improvements in some environments with this approach, it is not without its flaws.

First of all, if you centralize estimation, you might increase precision, but you definitely degrade accuracy. This team needs to be intimately familiar with all of the work; all systems, all requirements, all dependencies, all interactions. They need to achieve this level of understanding with limited, if not zero, hands on experience in the work they are estimating. The more time they spend reading requirements and estimating work for others to do, the less time they have to do the actual work. The less time they spend doing the actual work, the less accurate their estimations become. And the more teams they have to estimate for, the less time they have to prepare for each team, which further degrades accuracy.

Second of all, if you have a specific team that estimates then you still need a team that does the actual work. We'll call them the delivery team. The delivery team must also be intimately familiar with all of the work; all systems, all requirements, all dependencies, all interactions. This means both teams must do the work required to estimate. We've introduced a good deal of duplicate effort into the system while simultaneously degrading accuracy. This is pure waste.

Third of all, there are multiple factors to a team's ability to execute. Even when it is the same team performing all estimates, these factors come into play. We discussed variances in product roadmaps, backlogs, and stories when we talked about cross-team velocity comparisons. All of these variables still exist. Add in different specific technical factors and even when the same team performs estimates across all work, their own estimates will differ in accuracy across the differing projects. The increase in accuracy we were trying to achieve is still elusive.

Finally, the more burdened the estimating team, the more likely delivery teams need to wait - because we all know projects can't start until they're estimated. Now we have diminished accuracy, waste, and delays; all in exchange for the hopes that consistency in estimation will make up for the cost of centralization.

It won't.

# Estimating in Time

There are a number of problems related to estimating in time. From mistaking effort and duration as equivalent to an obsession with getting estimates "right", estimating in time tends to create too much focus on how long things take versus when things will be done.

If you must estimate, I say, estimate in abstractions. Abstractions away from time, such as points representing complexity or effort or whatever non-time thing you want to focus on, don't necessarily help make estimates any more accurate. They help by changing our focus and altering our expectations - all through obfuscation.

When we estimate in time, we compare in time. When we compare in time, we tend to get hung up on the measurement and ignore the statistics. We often pay more attention to whether or not each item took the time estimated and fail to pay sufficient attention to whether or not the data we've gathered is beneficial for forecasting.

Say you estimate stories in points as a relative measure of complexity. Over time, you discover that 3 points is approximately 31 hours of work. The mean is 31, the median is 31, and the mode is 29. There are obviously some outliers, but our standard deviation is only 3.27 with an entire range of approximately 27 to 35. We have data that informs us that an estimate of 3 points can usually be completed within a two week period. Armed with this and similar data on more and less complex stories, we can do a pretty good job of forecasting.

We can map this data on a simple cycle time control chart. From there, we can identify outliers and discuss them for learning. We can hone our precision within a reasonable range, understanding that ultimately, we are taking educated guesses at how complex a task we've never attempted before is going to be.

Estimating in points or some abstraction, we are more willing to accept the durations on face value. So long as the durations fall within a particular range, we are okay with the variance. If it turns out that 3 points equates to an average of 31 hours, cool. If 3 points equate to a duration of 7 days, cool.

When we estimate in time, something awful happens. Suddenly, the data is supposed to match a pre-determined expectation. If you say 3 days and the stories take 7 days to complete, we hone in on what we did wrong in estimating. There is some soft shaming, gnashing of teeth, and a ceremonial 5-why attack on each story that missed the estimate. "You need to get better at estimating", becomes a mantra.

But, it turns out that effort and duration are rarely correlated, much less equivalent. Such correlation only occurs on high process efficiency teams. For most teams, the correlation is weak or non-existent. This is due to the fact that most of what impedes the work is queues and system level impediments that are generally unrelated to the work. For organizations where issues exist such as extensive infrastructure lead times, limited stakeholder availability, or cross-team dependencies, there is almost no correlation of duration to the size of the work.

 Effort and duration are rarely correlated, much less equivalent

There are two considerations when it comes to estimating: accuracy and precision.

Accuracy is how close our estimate is to the true value, whereas, precision is how consistent the estimates are.

Let's assume we have a list of completed items and many of those items took 48 working hours to complete.

If we find that our original estimates on these items all fall within the range of 40 to 56, we can say we are pretty accurate. No estimate is off by more than 20% of the actual. We are, however, not very precise. The estimates have a range of 16, which is a pretty big spread relative to the actual work.

If, on the other hand, we find that our original estimates on these items all fall within the range of 32 to 34, we can say we are pretty precise. All of the estimates are off of the actual by a good amount, but they are within a very tight range.

Of course, in an ideal world, we'd want perfect accuracy (hit the bullseye) and precision (hit it every time). But if we have to choose between accuracy and precision, precision provides a tighter correlation to actual and allows us to better forecast. Unfortunately when we estimate in time, we tend to become focused on accuracy over precision.

## Comparing Estimates to Actuals

Many organizations seem to have an obsession with getting esti-mates "right". After all, we need to know when the project will be done. And we need accuracy. Knowing the entire project will be done before the end of the third quarter isn't good enough. We need to know that the project will be done this month or this week or perhaps even on this specific day.

 Through consistency, we attempt to achieve pre-dictability.

I've watched teams put a great deal of effort into improving their estimates. I've seen teams compare stories from this iteration to stories from prior iterations to try to maintain consistency. I've seen teams use a reference story for a single point. When estimating, they look at the reference story and then estimate all others compared to it. These seem like decent practices. The goal of these practices is consistency. Through consistency, we attempt to achieve predictability.

But one thing I've never understood is the notion of estimates versus actuals. Here we look at the original estimate for a story and we then estimate again once the story is complete. The idea here is that the estimate upon completion is an actual. Now if you're estimating in time, I suppose you could use the actual. If you're estimating in points that you equate to time, I still suppose you could use the actual. I still don't think it is a good idea, but I can see the logic in it. The real problem, in my opinion, is that you think you can estimate in time in the first place.

In this case, the practice I am referring to is when a team estimates complexity in points, completes the work, and sizes the story again based on what they've learned. This is supposed to provide a learning opportunity whereby we can improve our estimates going forward. This, to me, is a flawed approach. The assumption is that the next story that has unknown unknowns will be more knowable because we learned what we didn't know when we built this story. You following me here? Me neither.

To illustrate my point, let's look at estimations from a slightly different angle.

## Estimating Sudoku

Indulge me for a bit here. Writing code is really problem solving. Sudoku is (clearly) problem solving. Admittedly, sudoku is far more simple than writing code; simple in terms of strict constraints with very few possible solutions (often one solution). If we can agree that sudoku can serve as a simple model for writing code, then please do read on.

I have a sudoku game on my phone. It breaks the games down into four categories; easy, medium, hard, and expert. Clearly, the games are all on the same size grid with the exact same rules. The difference between these games is merely the number of seeded answers and their locations on the board. These two factors make a game more or less difficult to solve. I don't know that a medium is twice as difficult as an easy, but I am certain that a medium is more difficult than an easy.

# Actuals

I've played hundreds of sudoku games on my phone. I've played each level of difficulty at least 50 times. And the game has tracked my actual time to complete for every play. The following graph shows the time to complete for 40 games at each skill level. The y-axis is the time to complete. The x-axis is the number of games.

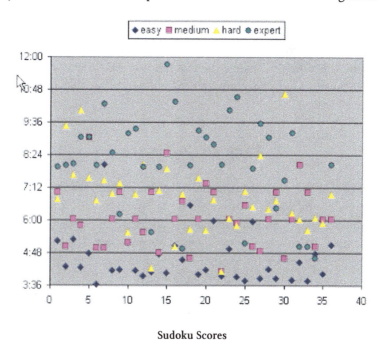

Sudoku Scores

At point 6 on the x axis, the easy story takes nearly 8 minutes to complete. This is well outside the normal effort for an easy. In fact, it exceeds the average for a medium. After completion of this puzzle, were you to have asked me why it took so long, I might have concluded that it was actually a medium or even a hard. But the truth is, it was an easy. For some reason, I struggled to solve it. Maybe I missed a subtle clue. Maybe I made a mistake that sent me down a wrong path for quite a while. I honestly don't recall. I might not even know why it took me so long. But the amount of effort it took me to determine the solution does not change the quality of the puzzle itself.

> It didn't become an easy puzzle just because I found it easy to solve.

Similarly, there are a number of times where I managed to complete expert puzzles in times consistent with a medium or even an easy. Again, this does not change the fact that the puzzle was an expert level puzzle. It didn't become an easy puzzle just because I found it easy to solve.

## Back to Software

Looking at the variance in simple sudoku puzzles, I hope we can agree the same kind of variance is perfectly reasonable in software development. An estimate of 1 point indicates the team agrees this is a story of relatively low complexity and that it is similar in complexity to other stories that we previously agreed were also 1 point. An estimate of 1 point does not directly indicate that it will take a specific amount of time (or less). An estimate of 1 point does not necessarily indicate that it will be faster to complete than a 2 point or 3 point story. On average, a 1 point story will be completed in less time than a 2 or 3. *On average.*

> A 3 point story doesn't become a 1 point story just because you completed it quickly.

There are times when a story changes. Say certain requirements are dropped or we discover that we'd already written some of the code months ago. I am sure there are other reasons. But just because a story took longer or shorter than the average time to complete similarly sized stories does not mean the story was improperly sized. A 3 point story doesn't become a 1 point story just because you completed it quickly.

# It's All Relative

If you have to estimate (you probably don't), then I recommend you use a reference story. Identify a story that the entire team can agree is 1 point. Identify a second story that the entire team can agree is 5 points. When you are estimating, keep these stories in mind and attempt to estimate all others relative to them. Then, at the end of the estimating session, compare the stories to one another and your reference models. Do the points still feel right? Compare the stories to random selections from prior iterations? Do the points still feel right? If not, make adjustments to your new estimates as necessary.

Common advice for relative sizing is to choose a story the entire team agrees is a 1 and use it as the reference point. The challenge with this approach is that the further from 1 you get, the harder it is to extrapolate from 1 and as a result, the entire set of point estimates tends to be compressed toward the lower end. By including a 5 point story, you have something on the mid to high end to use as an additional reference point, helping to extrapolate out further, if you need.

Better still, when you are done with all of these adjustments, take any story that is larger than the mean story size and try to break it down into smaller pieces that still deliver some amount of business value or learning. Continue this practice until all of your stories are within one point of the mean. And better still, break stories down into the smallest pieces you can conceive of that still offer some business value and assign them all a size of 1.

## Set it and Forget it

If you're going to estimate stories, don't keep tweaking those estimates. Once you've gone through the process of relative estimation, near-term comparison, and historical comparison, set the story points (or whatever unit of measure you fancy) and pretty much leave it. Learn something significant? Sure, make an adjustment. Complete change in technical direction? Sure, make an adjustment. But other than something major that materially influences the entire project, stop obsessing over sizing your stories. And stop fevering over actuals versus estimates. If you want those numbers to get closer to one another on a more consistent basis, focus instead on making your stories small enough that the variance is insignificant. At that point, by the way, there's definitely no need for estimates. So there's certainly no need to compare an estimate against an actual.

# Measuring Individual Velocity

I see this far more often than I'd like. Not only do we monitor a team's velocity, but we measure the velocity of each individual on the team; or at least each individual developer. Some of you are wondering why this is a problem.

If the team's velocity is the total work they complete in a given timeframe, then the sum of the individual velocity for each team member is the team velocity. It's probably good to know who is actually contributing and who needs improvement, right?

And therein lies the problem. On a healthy team, I want the lead developer delivering fewer points than the rest of the team. I want them taking time out to work on automation and standards. I want them to mentor other developers and to collaborate with other teams that we're dependent on. I want them thinking about architecture and jumping on the big problems when they arise. If we track individual velocity, we're telling everyone on the team that their individual performance is what matters. We're telling our lead not to work on all of these other important items that are better suited for her experience level. We're telling our lead to focus on picking up stories and getting them done, just like everybody else.

"Simple enough", you say, "give the lead special forgiveness."

Ah. Right. Only the plebeians should be measured and evaluated on personal velocity. Except we want them to pair sometimes, maybe even mob. We want them to share the work. We want them to work collectively. If a story gets started by one developer, but finished by another, who gets the credit for the velocity? If the story is completed by a pair, who gets the credit for the velocity? If the story is mobbed, who gets the credit? What about that system outage that turned into a three-day war room and pulled two of the developers away for an entire week? What do we do about their individual velocity?

Measuring individual velocity fails to give us a complete picture. It likely gives us the wrong impression. People who help others will likely have lower velocity numbers. People who get pulled off of story work to work on production issues will definitely have lower velocity numbers.

So, to recap: Measuring individual velocity won't tell you who is actually contributing to the team, who is improving process, or even who actually delivers the most stories, but it will encourage your team to make collaboration a secondary concern at best.

# Iteration Packing

I travel a lot for work. I mean a lot. I am away from home at least 70% of the time. Every week I travel away from home for several days, usually to a different state, sometimes to a different country.

I have a carry-on suitcase that was designed for international travel. I love it. It is smaller than most US carry-on bags, but it fits in the overhead of many planes; domestic and international, that won't accommodate other carry-ons. This is super convenient.

As you can imagine, I'm pretty experienced at packing a suitcase at this point. My daughter bought me some packing cubes a couple of years back and I've become adept at using them, which has only enhanced my ability to pack well for trips. I can go away for up to 6 days with this small suitcase and have sufficient clothes to wear for work and play, including shoes and clothes for working out.

But most of the time I travel, I am not away for 6 days. Most of the time, I am away for 4 or 5 days. Given my ability to fit 6 days of clothes into my suitcase, I always have a little extra room on these shorter trips. What I would really like is to take an extra pair of shoes. But my feet are big and my shoes take up a lot of room. There's no way I can get them in there, no matter how much I want them. So, invariably, I will decide to pack an extra couple of shirts, a book, or some other item that I *might* want on the trip. And as you might guess, I rarely if ever wear the extra shirts or read the book.

Then, while on the trip I'll find a treasure; some item I'd really like to have. Something that would be of value to me or to a family member. But I cannot make the purchase because there is not enough room in my suitcase.

I mean, what was I to do? The suitcase had room! I had to fill it. I couldn't leave for the trip without taking a few extras I might need when the suitcase was clearly not completely filled. I mean, what kind of person travels with a partially filled suitcase? That's just crazy. I'd rather lug around extra shirts and a book because to not lug them would be an inefficient use of the suitcase. A full suitcase is a happy suitcase.

And such is the attitude of many an agile team. A full iteration is a happy iteration.

Given an average velocity of 22, if the team has loaded up 19 points of valuable and pressing work into an iteration and the next most important story is 8 points, they'll search the backlog for a 3 point story or a combination of 1 and 2 point stories to fill the iteration to the maximum. They'll pack an iteration with lower-value items just to make sure the iteration is full. They'll lug around low value items that they probably won't get to and don't matter that much if they do get to them. They'll do this and forgo the opportunity to do other more valuable things.

Iteration packing seems harmless enough on the surface. There's room in the iteration, why not fill it? But it persists a focus on utilization over value. At best, you deliver stuff that doesn't matter as much. More likely what happens is you cannot fit late discovered items of value into the iteration. You leave no slack for production outages or escaped defects. And you leave no opportunity for things like learning and reduction of technical debt.

If you haven't built slack into your process anywhere else, then this is the place to do so. If you think you've built slack into the process, but didn't do it deliberately or your Cumulative Flow Diagram tells you the slack is immediately after a bottleneck, you don't have actual slack. If you don't have slack, definitely don't pack your iterations. Leave a bit of room for serendipity or even misfortune. Instead of packing the iteration, provide the team the opportunity to pull in more work as capacity allows. This also creates space for other care and feeding of the system and source code. It additionally allows the team to feel good about pulling in extra work when possible rather than feeling bad about not achieving 100% of a velocity goal per iteration.

# Potential Side Effects of Metrics

Now, metrics are not bad. But, they are often used in bad ways.

It might help to be aware of some of the side effects of mismanagement of metrics. From inadvertently creating behaviors that actively work against our best interest, to altering the meaning of the metric, mismanagement can do more harm than good.

## The Hawthorne Effect

Western Electric had commissioned an extensive study that ran from 1924 to 1932 at their Hawthorne Works in Cicero, IL.[10] The intent of the study was to determine the impact of ambient lighting on worker productivity. Would employees be more productive under high levels of light or low levels of light? The workers in the factory were divided into two groups based on physical location within the plant. For one group, the lighting was increased dramatically while for the other group (the control) lighting levels remained the same. Researchers found that productivity improved among the group for whom lighting changed whereas the control group had no statistically significant change.

Employee working conditions were then changed in other ways. Working hours were adjusted, rest breaks were changed, floors were rearranged, workstations were kept cleaner, and several other adjustments were made, including returning the lighting back to

[10]The "Hawthorne Effect". (n.d.). Retrieved January 18, 2018, from https://www.library.hbs.edu/hc/hawthorne/09.html

normal levels and changing practices and policies back to original standards.

With every change, productivity made small improvements. By early 1932, and the end of the studies, the factory productivity was at an all-time high and employee attendance and retention were at record-setting levels. Some groups seemed to do better than others, but across the factory, all measures were improved.

When the studies ended, productivity, attendance, and retention soon returned to original levels.

The key takeaway from the Hawthorne studies is - that which gets measured will improve, at least temporarily. "The Hawthorne Effect" is described as the phenomenon in which subjects in behavioral studies change their performance in response to being observed.

This, at first, seems like a precious nugget of management gold.

1. Measure productivity.
2. Make it known.
3. Ka-Pow! Increased productivity.

The perfect management formula.

But the reality was (and is), that while that which is being measured shows improvement, it does not mean the overall system has improved. Working longer hours can lead to employee fatigue and burn out, as well as lower quality output and thereby lower quality outcomes. Lack of attention in areas not measured, such as quality or workplace safety, can lead to other negative outcomes.

If your team is slacking so significantly that merely measuring their velocity can result in a marked increase in velocity with no ill-effects, then you've a more serious issue at play than velocity.

What's more, there is no guarantee that the thing being measured has actually improved. Velocity might have gone up because the team inflated story points. We should rephrase the key takeaway to that which gets measured will **appear to** improve.

 That which gets measured will **appear to** improve.

# Goodhart's Law

Charles Goodhart is an economist and former advisor to the Bank of England. In 1975, Goodhart delivered two papers to a conference at the Reserve Bank of Australia.[11] In those papers, Goodhart was discussing research and theory related to monetary policy and control in the United Kingdom. In the years leading up to 1975, existing monetary targets and the controls used to achieve the goals were no longer producing the results desired or expected. There had been what most considered to be evidence of a stable money demand in the United Kingdom. It was believed that the growth of money could be controlled through the setting of short-term interest rates. Higher interest rates correlated with lower money growth.

Goodhart warned, however, that policies and practices based on specific targets were flawed. Goodhart stated,

 "Any statistical regularity will tend to collapse once pressure is placed upon it for control purposes."

A common paraphrasing is, "When a measure becomes a target, it

---

[11]Crystal, K. Alec, and Paul D Mizen. "Goodhart's Law: Its Origins, Meaning and Implications for Monetary Policy," November 12, 2001. https://cyberlibris.typepad.com/blog/files/Goodharts_Law.pdf.

ceases to be a good measure."[12] When I talk about this, I tend to add, "And the target therefore no longer means what you think it does."

Goodhart's law is a critical piece of information when we think about metrics. No matter how tempting it might be, the moment we set a target for a measure, we've changed the system, thereby changing what the measurement means, thereby changing what the target means.

The lesson here is pretty simple. Don't set targets for metrics. And please don't give teams incentives towards targets if you do set them. I know. I know. Management 101 says this works. But, science says it doesn't[13]. Seriously. Setting targets and providing incentives for knowledge work lowers performance. Don't do it.

Instead, provide guidelines to the teams. My favorite guideline for metrics is, "Monitor trending. Dig in when the trend changes and you aren't absolutely certain why."

## Friedman's Thermostat

Milton Friedman was an award winning economist who, among other things, served as advisor to President Ronald Reagan.

In an article published in The Wall Street Journal in August of 2003, Friedman stated, "The contrast between the periods before and after the middle of the 1980s is remarkable. Before, it is like a chart of the temperature in a room without a thermostat in a location with very variable climate; after, it is like the temperature in the same room but with a reasonably good though not perfect thermostat, and one that is set to a gradually declining temperature. Sometime around

[12]"Goodhart's Law." Wikipedia. Wikimedia Foundation, October 21, 2017. https://en.wikipedia.org/wiki/Goodhart's_law#Formulation.

[13]Deci, E. L., Koestner, R., & Ryan, R. M. (1999, November). A meta-analytic review of experiments examining the effects of extrinsic rewards on intrinsic motivation. Retrieved August 19, 2017, from https://www.ncbi.nlm.nih.gov/pubmed/10589297

1985, the Fed appears to have acquired the thermostat that it had been seeking the whole of its life."[14]

The article continues on to explain that the real cause of the improvement was a change in the way the Federal Reserve approached their role in regard to price stability. Prior to the 1980s, Keynesian Economics, the dominant theory of the times, taught economists that the volume of money did not matter in the control of price stability as there was no correlation between volume and price. But this theory was disproven as shown by performance in the 1970s and 1980s. New Keynesian Economics now includes quantity as part of the theory.

Rather than get any further into the details of economic theory, which I am grossly disqualified to do, I thought it better to explain Friedman's Thermostat with a parable of my own - involving a thermostat.

## The Case Against Thermostats

Imagine for a moment, that you are the ruler of a sovereign province. The people are happy under your rule. There is plenty of food to go around, everyone has meaningful work that contributes to the overall health and wellbeing of the people. There is time for leisure and your people want for very little. If there were one wish, one thing the people would like, it would be for the winters to be less harsh. Summers in the land are wonderful with long comfortable days, lush green lands, and blue skies. Spring and fall are equally beautiful in their varying colors and the cooler, but comfortable temperatures. But winter is harshly cold and the days are short. A mere three months out of twelve, the winters are nearly insufferable. The nights may be long, but sleep is hard to come by. Families must take shifts tending to the fire and everyone must huddle together in the main room to keep warm; man and pet.

---

[14]MiltonFriedman. "The Fed's Thermostat." The Wall Street Journal. Dow Jones & Company, August 19, 2003. https://www.wsj.com/articles/SB106125694925954100.

One day, you hear of a land three days ride away where the people do not suffer through the winter. A land where despite the cold, the homes are warm throughout. These people have a mysterious device in every household that they call the "thermostat". These thermostats, small dials on the wall, somehow allow the people of this land to keep their homes at whatever temperature they desire throughout the winter.

Curious, and hopeful that such a magical device might work in your own homes, you send a small party to visit the land and to learn about these thermostats. They are instructed to observe these people and their devices, gather data, and devise a plan for how your land can best solve the challenge of harsh winters. The party takes off just as the leaves are starting to turn vibrant; the first warning of winter's approach.

Weeks pass and the fall turns to winter and the winter grows more bitter, but you hold faith that the research party will return and provide answers. As the worst of winter seems to be over, the party returns, riding hard to the gates.

"We've news, your highness, of the utmost urgency. We've ridden practically straight through."

You can see they are worn and weary from long days and short nights.

"Have you made adequate observations to understand what is happening?", you ask to the head of the party, a chief scientist who has taken sabbatical from the university to make this trip.

"We have.", they answer.

"And", you inquire in anticipation, "do you have a clear plan for how we might ease the bitter winters?"

"We do...", they reply hesitantly.

"Well, waste not another minute!", you exclaim impatiently, "Tell me. What is your plan?"

Calmly, carefully, and crisply, as though to ensure you do not mishear, they state, "We must go to war with them. We must stop them."

"What?", you inquire, puzzled and thinking that you must have misheard, "Go to war? Stop them from what? What have you learned?"

A little more rushed this time, accidentally confessing a sense of anxiety, they continue, "Well, you see, your highness, we observed for many weeks the activities of these people and their strange devices. We learned that rather than burning wood, they burn a type of liquid they call fuel. This fuel is drawn from the ground and distributed to each of the homes. So we had three things to observe; the inside temperature, the outside temperature, and the amount of fuel they consumed."

"And what did you find?", you ask, frustrated at how long this is taking; you would not wage war, risking people's lives, over trivial matters and fuel and temperature readings are trivial matters, "How is it that we must wage war to make our homes comfortable in winter?"

"Well, your highness,", they reply, once again calm and measured, "after careful observation, we determined a few things."

"Again, there were three things to measure; Inside Temperature, Outside Temperature, and Fuel Consumed."

If rolling your eyes were dignified in the least, you'd do it right now.

"First, your highness, we observed that the temperature in the home remained comfortable throughout the winter. In fact, the home temperature fluctuated only slightly. Small enough that the fluctuation fell within a reasonable margin of error. For all intents and purposes, the temperature of the home remained constant."

"That is the point.", you think to yourself, putting a great deal of effort into being patient. "Are all scientists this long-winded?"

"Second, we observed that both the outside temperature and the fuel consumption varied significantly."

"Upon further analysis of the data, we found no correlation between the outside temperature and the inside temperature of the home. We also found no correlation between the fuel consumption and the temperature in the home. No matter the measure of either of these two factors, the home remained at a constant temperature. We did, however, confirm a tight negative correlation between the fuel consumption and the outside temperature. Higher fuel consumption correlated to lower outside temperatures."

"Is this true?", you ask. Shocked at the findings.

"It is your highness.", they reply with pride.

And then in a faster tempo, excited to tell you the rest of the story, they continue, "We thought it odd at first. These variables are not logically correlated. But when we stepped back and took a look at the whole system, we realized what was happening."

"You recall when I mentioned the fuel and how it is extracted from the ground?" They ask but do not wait for an answer and instead continue on. "We arrived in late summer, observed that after they started to draw fuel from the ground in late summer, the temperatures started to drop. And the more fuel they drew, the colder it got. Eventually, it got so cold, their equipment wouldn't work and they could no longer draw fuel from the ground. Sure enough, within a matter of days, temperatures started to rise again."

"Realizing that it is the draw of fuel from the ground that lowers the surface temperature, which makes the frost, which lowers the air temperature, which causes the winter, we had to stop them from drawing any more fuel. But we were unable to convince them, your highness. Despite all of our data and the obvious connections. Despite our years of scientific study and mastery, they refused to accept our findings and insisted on continuing their dangerous practices."

"If we want winter to end, we must stop them from drawing any more fuel. We must wage war!"

# The Lessons of Friedman's Thermostat

There are numerous lessons one could draw from this tale, but we are focused on two.

## Correlation is Not Causation

The first is best expressed through a common phrase, "Correlation is not causation." Observing a correlation between two items doesn't necessarily inform us which caused the other, if they've such a relationship at all.

In our story, the chief scientist concludes that the draw of fuel from the ground is causing dropping temperatures. But we know, of course, that the knowledge of an impending increase in demand due to lowering temperatures is what causes the extraction of more fuel.

In other cases, it may be that there is no cause/effect relationship at all and the correlation may be purely coincidental. Take, for example, the per capita consumption of beef in the US from 2000 through 2009 and the number of deaths by lightning during that same time period.[15] The two are clearly positively correlated. This in no way suggests that either caused the other. This is a coincidental correlation and any conclusions drawn therefrom are dubious.

---

[15]"Per Capita Consumption of Beef (US) Correlates with Deaths Caused by Lightning." Spurious Correlations, n.d. http://tylervigen.com/view_correlation?id=1476.

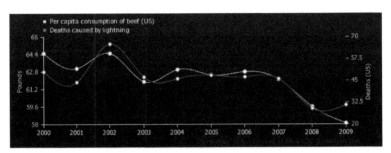

US Per Capita Consumption of Beef correlates to Death by Lightning

## No Correlation Doesn't Imply There's No Causation

The second lesson, and the purpose of Friedman's original thermo-stat metaphor, was to emphasize that there are cases under which, without a comprehensive understanding of the system, one might conclude through measurement that correlations do not exist when they do in fact exist. This misread of the system can further lead us to completely overlook present cause and effect.

In our story, the constant temperature in the house indicated there was no correlation between the outside temperature and that of the home. Nor was there a correlation between the fuel consumed and the temperature of the home. This conclusion was supported by the measurements, but only in as much as the scientists did not understand the entire system. The furnace (in partnership with the thermostat) kept the internal temperature regulated such that the actual cause and effect and the actual correlation between the internal and external temperature, were indiscernible.

In Friedman's case, the Federal Reserve had long operated under Keynesian Economic theory and ignored the impact of volume on price stability. Keynesian theories were developed at a time when measurements indicated no correlation between volume and price. The formulas developed at the time were, naive, but worked so long as the system stayed in a particular balance. Throughout the 70s that balance was lost, along with the correlation, and thereby the cause and effect relationship was revealed.

# Perverse Incentives

A perverse incentive is any incentive that creates an impact counter to the intended outcome.

Take, for example, a call center that receives complaints from customers that resolution takes too long and they spend too much time on the phone. A well-intentioned manager announces a new program wherein call center agents who manage to lower their average call time are rewarded. The outcome is, in fact, lower call times. Three months later, new customer surveys indicate that problems take longer to solve because customers are now instructed to call back in 30 minutes rather than waiting on hold for 5 minutes. This allows agents the time to do the research necessary while keeping average call times down. It is a poorer customer experience, but call times went down and bonuses were paid.

Now, what about in software?

Let's say the quality control manager wants to lower the number of defects released into production. They sincerely want better quality software released to customers more often. In an effort to entice analysts to up their game, the manager decides to run a program where analysts are rewarded for finding more bugs. The end result is a dramatic increase in bugs reported prior to production release. More time in a given iteration is now spent discussing whether or not the increase of reported defects are in fact the same defect reported multiple times or genuinely distinct defects, whether or not something is actually a missed requirement or a defect, and whether or not the credit should go to the analyst who reported it first or to the one who determined how it could be recreated. In the end, fewer defects are released with each push to production. But so are fewer features.

Several years back, I was working with a client and we'd implemented some code quality metrics. We were using them as part of the team's retrospectives and planning. We'd look at trending on the metrics and discuss whether or not this was what we expected and if we should adjust our planning as a result. Was quality dropping while throughput was going up? Was this acceptable? Should we make adjustments?

This went well for a few months. Eventually, someone in a position of authority decided that the code coverage metric was important. Important enough that it should go up. We should release better quality software and code coverage would help to assure that quality was high. So they announced a bonus for the team if the code coverage increased from approximately 35% to 100% before the end of the year.

Now this was a legacy system. It had 0% coverage when the team took it over. The 35% was achieved by writing tests around new behavior and character testing anything that they needed to update. So all tests were around code that had been changing for business purposes. With this new program, now all code would need to be covered.

Months rolled by and the team did their best to sneak in coverage on code they wouldn't have otherwise touched, but they primarily focused on work that added value to the customer. Come November, they were only at about 60% coverage. It wasn't lookin' good.

Then, over the Thanksgiving holiday, a miracle happened. The last check-in on Wednesday showed 62% coverage. Everybody went home for the long weekend.

Come Monday morning, on first check-in, the continuous integration server kicked off the tests and reported 100% code coverage. A 38% increase over the holiday weekend. Bonuses were going to be paid!

Upon further investigation, it was found that a member of the team spent a little time over the weekend and, using reflection, had written a test that exercised every branch of the code and then asserted that true was equal to true. As it turns out, true is always equal to true. The test passed. A fake test that fooled the system and, technically, met the requirement for bonus payout.

As you might guess, bonuses were not paid.

You might agree this is an unfortunate story, but how was it a perverse incentive? The team spent months trying to write tests against code that they were not changing in an effort to get to 100% coverage. This effort distracted from core work. The measurable quality of the code did not increase. In fact, it went down. Refactoring was pushed aside in exchange for writing tests. Barely working was good enough for new features. They had tests to write.

The intent was to ensure the team was releasing better quality code. But it did no such thing. It ultimately distracted from the efforts that would have actually resulted in better quality code.

# Variable Velocity

Have you ever been on a team where your velocity suffered wild variances? Maybe you ended up using a running average instead of yesterday's weather?

Have you heard phrases like, "Well, our velocity last iteration was 3, but our average is still 22."?

Have you ever heard the phrase, "Dude, we need to get this velocity stable."?

Have you worked on teams where they took partial credit for done at the end of the iteration? Where maybe you'd split a card strictly on points and award some apportion to the current iteration and assign the remainder of the card to the next iteration?

## Velocity Should Stabilize

It seems much of what we read tells us that velocity will do two things: stabilize and improve. According to CollabNet/VersionOne, we can expect that velocity will stabilize within three to six months[16]. James Shore's "The Art of Agile" tells us to give it three or four iterations to stabilize.[17]

---

[16]"Measuring the Velocity of Your Agile Scrum Team." Agile Scrum Velocity Calculation & FAQs, September 26, 2018. https://resources.collab.net/agile-101/agile-scrum-velocity.

[17]Shore, James. "The Art of Agile" James Shore: The Art of Agile Development: Estimating, n.d. https://www.jamesshore.com/Agile-Book/estimating.html.

# But What If Velocity Doesn't Stabilize?

First, take a deep breath, then repeat the following three times:

*Unstable velocity is a symptom.*
*Unstable velocity is not a diagnosis.*

Velocity lets us know something about the team's performance; it is a health indicator, if you will. An unstable velocity might indicate a team health issue, but it doesn't give us sufficient information to diagnose the actual cause. And it might be that this team is in perfectly fine health, despite an unstable velocity.

Think of velocity as heart rate. An abnormal heart rate, be it too fast, too slow, or irregular, can indicate a number of underlying issues such as electrolyte imbalance, overstimulation, insufficient rest, autoimmune disorders, thyroid problems, or various forms of heart disease. Or maybe you simply have an abnormal heart rate and are actually a healthy individual. An abnormal heart rate indicates a possible problem. And your problem is not an abnormal heart rate.

An erratic velocity can indicate a number of underlying issues such as poor story composition, dependencies on other teams or individuals, too much work in progress, silos, and various forms of mismanagement. Or maybe you simply have an erratic velocity and are actually a healthy team. An erratic velocity indicates a possible problem. And your problem is not an erratic velocity.

Whatever the underlying problem, it is something you can adjust. Adjustments for which you can observe the outcome. But the important thing to remember is that the velocity is not the problem. Do not try to fix the velocity. Try to figure out what it is telling you and fix that.

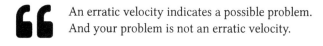

An erratic velocity indicates a possible problem. And your problem is not an erratic velocity.

If an erratic velocity could be telling you any number of things, then how do you know what to adjust? Ask your team. They probably know. They may not know they know, but they can give you indicators.

Let's look through some of the common underlying causes.

# Poor Story Composition

By story composition, I mean story size and dependencies.

The larger the story, the more risk there is of getting it to done. But it is not just about making stories small. It is about making them small and independent. Small stories that cannot be delivered independent of one another are really just tasks for a large story.

If we have an issue with proper story composition, we may find we get several stories close to done, but we cannot run acceptance tests on them until all of them are complete, leaving us with too much testing at the end of the iteration. If we don't get all of the stories ready for acceptance testing, none of them can move. Then, next iteration, we complete the last strays and a glut of cards/points move to done. Alternatively, some stories are just too big to complete in a single iteration.

There is no need to get your stories perfect up front. Get them good enough to do high-level planning; think epics. Then as you start planning releases, break them down into features to get a finer-course roadmap. Finally, as you plan iterations, break them down again into small, independently deliverable items.

Beware the temptation to split stories across technical seams. This is often the way we think about the work because it is the way we anticipate the work being executed. We know for this feature that we need some database changes, so that becomes a story. We additionally make separate stories for changes to the API and changes to the user interface. We might even break the user interface into design and logic. But what we've done is create three or four stories that cannot be independently delivered. They're all connected. They are one story.

Instead, focus on small stories that are thin vertical slices through the technology stack. Now that's easy enough to say and it sounds right, but it is not necessarily that easy to execute on. Sometimes, thin vertical slices look like waste. They cause us to build something less than what we'd envisioned. And we don't want to release anything less than perfect, do we?

 Focus on small stories that are thin vertical slices through the technology stack.

I find it interesting how many teams I work with will simultaneously push for a Minimum Viable Product (MVP) and insist it is the right way to bring a piece of software to the market while arguing that writing a simpler version of the code is a waste of time since we already know what we need. An MVP is about learning: learning if what you *thought* the customer wanted was, in fact, what they wanted. An MVP is about getting something out there to validate your hypothesis and to learn. In that regard, thin vertical slices are merely MVPs taken to the next level.

## Thin Slices - An Example

Let's take a look at a relatively simple example wherein a team needs to add search capability to a catalog of products. The product owner delivers a set of mock ups and a set of specifications that detail the desired functionality.

According to the specification, we want a search bar in the header of every page on the site. The bar will be hidden, but will appear just below the header when a search icon is pressed. After three keystrokes a search assist box should appear, showing possible matches to the search criteria. A user can continue to type or can select an item from the search assist box. So, for example, the site is for shoes and the user types in "mar". The search result box should show Doc Martens, Marc Joseph, Mark Lemp, Smartwool, and Tamaris. The user adds a "t" to the end of the text and Doc Martens and Smartwool should be the only options. The items in the search assist box should have a thumbnail, the brand name, and a brief description.

If we iterate our way toward the objective, we reduce our risk, increase our options, and create opportunities for learning. I'd start with a simple search page. The search icon on the home page would navigate to a new page with a simple search box and a submit (or search) button. The user types in what they want and clicks the button. A new page loads with their results in a simple list format. This list format is the contents we eventually want in the search assist box.

 If we iterate our way toward the objective, we reduce our risk, increase our options, and create opportunities for learning.

This works. If we decide to launch it, we now have search on the site. Along the way, we figured out things like connection to the database, the fundamental search capability, and how we might want to display the items. We also get to see how responsive the database is and think a bit more about what we'd expect to get back as our search results. If we choose to, we can launch this and gather statistics on how people are actually using search. What if they don't search by brand very often and instead search by model, or color, or purpose?

In the next increment, we might work on taking the form from a full request to an ajax call. We could leave the call tied to the submit button, but update the page based on the ajax call results. This allows us to get a better sense of the speed. Does the page update instantaneously or does it take a couple of seconds? What causes the delay - is it the database, the images, or something else? What do we need to do to get this to instantaneous?

In the next increment, perhaps we'd work on optimizations until the page refresh is as fast as we can get it - ideally milliseconds. Maybe we need to use a caching technique. Maybe there is a different search technology we can leverage. Do we need to alter our approach when there are 100 search results versus 10, 1, or 0?

In the next increment, we could switch the page to a type-ahead and remove the search button. Now, as people type, the results are shown in a search assist box and when they make a selection, they are redirected to the appropriate page. How does the search assist box feel? How do we navigate the search assist box with the keyboard? Can they press enter to go to the product page?

Now, in the last increment, we'd move the search box to the page header and wire up the functionality we want for hiding and showing the search bar.

You could break this down differently. Maybe you'd work on optimization after it launched and saw how it performed at scale. That's cool. Maybe you can think of seven increments. But in this example, we broke it down into five independent steps.

And along the way, we figured out a number of things. Each of them was relatively easy to solve, due in part to the fact that we worked on one thing at a time. We didn't try to get search, type-ahead, and optimization done all in one step. We had opportunities along the way to play with the interface, to maybe see how customers used it, and make adjustments. And every step was a deliverable, working piece of code.

Many developers will tell you this is a waste of time. They'll have to touch the same code multiple times. They'll have to change the code as they move along. The techniques we use for a basic web page are different from the techniques we use for a series of ajax calls. Why not just write it once instead of wasting all this time?

 You see, when we opt for all or nothing, the odds are always in favor of nothing.

Because none of this was time wasted. There were a number of things to figure out along the way. Some of them we had to figure out by writing the code and analyzing performance. Some of them we had to figure out by using the system. We want to expand our options and expedite our learning. Delivering in increments does both of these things quite well.

Many product owners will tell you that nothing but the final version is acceptable. If we don't get it right, the customer will hate it and they will run screaming to the competition to never, ever return. But when we hit the target date, there isn't a product owner alive who would want nothing to show rather than having some options to choose from. You see, when we opt for all or nothing, the odds are always in favor of nothing.

Thinking about the work in increments can lead to well-composed, thinly-sliced stories.

# Dependencies on Other Teams or Individuals

Perhaps your product owner is not available often enough and there is too much re-work due to slow feedback cycles. Maybe you don't have rights to your various environments and code migrations are executed in durations of days rather than minutes. It's possible some other technical team is not able to be as responsive or relies on process more than interactions for the exchange of information. Whatever it might be, any point where you need to wait for extended periods of time is likely to lead to other problems. For example, you can't sit idle, so you grab another card to work on, leading to too much work in process.

## Reduce Minutia

For things like approvals and code migrations, perhaps there is an opportunity to add some automation to expedite things.

When it comes to approvals, many places require wet signatures (actual ink) to indicate an approval. Some places require multiple signatures. This requirement is a throw-back to six month release cycles, lack of trust, antiquated documentation policies, and concerns over the legal acceptance of e-signatures. Those issues are all behind us, if we choose to allow them to be. With a little discipline, we can release code every single day; even multiple times per day. And with those more frequent releases, we've more opportunities to build trust. When it comes to documentation and signatures, there are plenty of secure e-signature tools that allow for cloud or on-premises storage of identities and signatures. In the US, if you are in a regulated industry, take a solid look at the regulations. You may find that there are no signature requirements whatsoever. For many other regulations, they refer to 21 CFR Part 11[18] compliance.

For code migrations, there are any number of tools available for creating a continuous delivery pipeline. These tools will allow you to set rules for migrations. To go from the Development environment to User Acceptance Testing (UAT), for example, the rules might be that the build has to complete, all unit tests pass, and the automated acceptance tests pass. To go from UAT to Quality Assurance (QA), perhaps the rules are that the build completes,

---

[18]"CFR 21 Part 11." ECFR - Code of Federal Regulations, https://www.ecfr.gov/cgi-bin/text-idx?node=pt21.1.11&rgn=div5.

all unit and acceptance tests pass, all regression tests pass, and an authorized user has signed off.

These examples are not recommendations, but merely common sets of rules I've seen in various environments. I'm not advocating for having multiple environments with sign-offs. I'm saying that if you do have such a situation, automate as much of it as you can.

Work with these teams and individuals on ways to automate processes, or find other ways to reduce their response time. Invite sponsors and others to your stand-ups, iteration planning, and retrospectives. If they consistently don't show, see if you can get another representative. Be professional and courteous, but there is no need to be completely deferent. If the project is important, you should be able to ask for the necessary support.

## Join Forces

It is not always possible to join forces, but it is often more possible than we think.

If you have common dependencies between teams, consider forming a single team. Maybe this is merging the two teams into one. Maybe this is creating a third team with members from each of the dependent teams. Maybe there are more than two teams involved.

 Talking, sharing, explaining, and solving together nets better overall results than maximizing the local efficiency of each individual or team.

By putting people together on a team to solve a specific business problem that crosses their typical boundaries, you eliminate most of the delays and miscommunication that normally happens. Despite the team members now moving "slower" because they're talking and sharing and explaining things and solving together, the project actually gets done faster. It turns out that talking, sharing, explaining, and solving together nets better overall results than maximizing the local efficiency of each individual or team.

If you can't come together as a single team focused on a key need, you can at least make a concerted effort to work with one another as directly as possible.

If you find that you are regularly joining forces between the same teams, this is a clear indicator that your organization is not organized well to meet the actual business needs. Listen to these clues. You'll find that if your department isn't properly structured, then your architecture probably won't be either. These mismatches become a vicious cycle. Your architecture will reinforce your organizational structure and your organizational structure will reinforce your architecture. If you want to change one, you must necessarily change the other.

In 1967, Melvin Conway submitted a paper[19] to the Harvard Business Review, which was rejected at the time for lack of evidence. In that paper, he stated, "Any organization that designs a system (defined broadly) will produce a design whose structure is a copy of the organization's communication structure."

Some time later, in the book, "The Mythical Man Month", Fred Brooks referenced Conway's thesis and coined it as "Conway's Law"[20]

Since then, studies performed by MIT and Harvard[21] have shown Conway to have been correct. The structure of our systems reflect the structure of our organizations.

If you want to change the design of the system (the architecture),

[19]Committees        Paper.        Accessed        October        19,        2018. http://www.melconway.com/Home/Committees_Paper.html.

[20]"Demystifying Conway's Law." ThoughtWorks. June 30, 2014. Accessed May 17, 2018. https://www.thoughtworks.com/insights/blog/demystifying-conways-law.

[21]Maccormack, Alan, John Rusnak, and Carliss Y. Baldwin. "Exploring the Duality between Product and Organizational Architectures: A Test of the Mirroring Hypothesis." SSRN Electronic Journal, 2008. https://doi.org/10.2139/ssrn.1104745.

you must change the design of the organization to reflect the desired outcome.

# Too Much Work In Process

Having too much Work in Process, also known as Work in Progress, is a remarkably common issue. In my experience, management often encourages this behavior. I don't know if it is the notion that we will get more done if we work on more things simultaneously, or perhaps there is a fear we won't get enough things done unless we work on several of them at once.

But what happens when we try to work on a few stories each? Remarkably, we make progress on several, but complete precious few. The more work in flow, the more context switching we all need to make. Coordination of the stories complicates testing and migrations. We look busy, but at the end of the iteration, we've fewer things complete. Then, at the beginning of the next iteration, a glut of work moves to done, setting us up with a couple day delay wrapping up the prior iteration and pushing us into yet another complicated cycle.

Drive each card to completion before picking up the next one. If a card is blocked, make getting it un-blocked a priority rather than letting it wait three days because George on the DBA team has a three-day SLA.

## You Cannot Multitask Complex Tasks

Even when we break our work down into small chunks, we have a certain cognitive load that comes with the work. - There's the purpose of the work: What is it for? Why do we need it now? - There's the requirements of the work: What is this supposed to look like? How is it supposed to behave? - There's the context of the work: What systems does this rely on? What systems do or will rely on it? Who is the customer? - There's the history of the work: Who has already worked on this? What got us to this point?

That's but a subset of the things we need to know about a work item when we pick it up. Each time we pick it up. *Every time* we pick it up.

The more work items you are "actively" working on, the more times you have to dump the cache of a prior work item and load the details of the current into your limited immediate recall. Even if you know the system well, there is a tax incurred. This tax is what we refer to as a context switch and it is pretty expensive.

Even for tasks that we are familiar with, there is a context switch when moving from one to the other. The more complex the tasks, the greater the cost. The cost of these switches can be significant; 20% per additional task on average with some studies showing as high as 40% per additional task[22].

Now some of you will argue that this cannot be true. If a context switch cost 20%, then a human could never work on more than five items at a time because they'd be 100% utilized, right?

Not exactly.

This isn't a utilization cost, it is a throughput cost. For every additional item you work on, you extend the duration of each item by 20%. So if you're working on two items, each of which would have taken two days, for a total of four days work, you will now complete the same work in 4.8 days. You effectively lost an entire day by attempting to work on two items in order to get things done "faster".

Also be aware that the cost is compounded. Two items is a 20% increase in the duration for both items. Add a third item and you increase the duration of all items by an additional 20% on top of

---

[22]Multitasking: Switching costs (n.d.). Retrieved February 24, 2017, from http://www.apa.org/research/action/multitask.aspx

the original 20%. So three items that normally take two days each wouldn't take six days, or even 7.2 days, but would take 8.16. Five items at two days effort each would require not 10 days to complete, but would require 17.03 days.

Let's take a look at a formula that we can use as a simple model. Assuming each task has the same duration, were it executed singularly, we can use a basic future value calculation for an investment[23].

```
1  d*(1+i)^(t-1) + d*(((1+i)^(t-1)-1)/i)*(1+i)
2
3  Where:
4
5  d = Duration of tasks
6  i = rate of increase as a decimal
7  t = count of tasks
```

Using this formula, we can see how I came up with 17.03 days.

```
1  d = 2, i = .2, t = 5
2
3  2*(1+.2)^(5-1) + 2*(((1+.2)^(5-1)-1)/.2)*(1+.2)
4  2*1.2^4 + 2*((1.2^4-1)/.2)*1.2
5  2*2.0736 + 2*((2.0736-1)/.2)*1.2
6  4.1472 + 2*(1.0736/.2)*1.2
7  4.1472 + 2*5.368*1.2
8  4.1472 + 12.8832
9  17.0304
```

So, yes, you can have seven or eight items in flight all at once and be super busy. Just know that you are also incredibly less efficient, and likely less effective.

[23]Hazell, A. (n.d.). Future Value Formula - Explained. Retrieved September 24, 2017, from http://www.thecalculatorsite.com/articles/finance/future-value-formula.php

# WIP, Throughput, and Little's Law

So, our future value calculation is both informative and interesting, but it is not particularly useful beyond making the point that doing more at once takes more time. What we want to know is how does this materially impact our ability to make software. For that, we can look to a more simple (and useful) calculation based on Little's Law[24]

Little's Law can be stated in a number of ways:

WIP = Throughput x Lead Time

WIP is the Work in Process. Lead Time is the time it takes for an item to get through the system. Throughput is the number of items a system can deliver in a given period of time.

So, let's say we have 5 items in process at the moment. And we have a Lead Time of 4 days with a 100% probability.

```
1   WIP = 5i
2   Throughput = T
3   Lead Time = 4d
4
5   5i = T x 4d
6
7   T = 5i/4d
8
9   T = 1.25 Items / Day
```

Based on the data we have about the system, we can assume these 5 items will take 4 days on average to clear the system. With this simple piece of information, we can project completion dates for any given item in the queue. Say, for example, there are still 5 items in WIP and we want to know about a story that is 10 items down

---

[24]Little's       Law.      Retrieved      March      14,      2017,      from
http://web.mit.edu/sgraves/www/papers/Little's%20Law-Published.pdf

in the backlog. That particular story, while not as high in value as the stories ahead of it has a due date 7 days from now. So while it is not as important, it is now more urgent.

Our target story is 15th in line when we include the items in process. 15i / 1.25i/d = 12d

Consequently, it is likely to be delivered in 12 days. We know that it is very likely going to be 5 days too late.

So let's target our item for 7 days from now.

```
1   Ni / 1.25i/d = 7d
2   Ni = 7d * 1.25i/d
3   N = 8.75
```

We can't have something at a three-quarter point in a queue, so in order to get it done 7 days from now, we'd need it to be 8th in the queue, including the current work in process. So it will need to be 3rd in the backlog. We can now determine if this is both desirable and feasible. Do we want to bump other items to a later delivery date? Can we deliver this before other stories or is it dependent on some of them? If it is dependent on some of them, can we bump them to positions one and two in the backlog to make this happen?

What if we are comfortable with something less than a 100% probability? What if we are good with a probability that indicates usually, but not always?

Let's say that 80% of our lead times are at or before 3 days. If we are comfortable with 80% probability, then we run the math again. Based on a lead time of 3 days, we determine that the throughput is 1.67 items per day and our item will be done in 9 days. At 80% probability, we'd need to move it to 11th in line, or 6th in the backlog. Remember, we always need to account for the work in process in addition to the work in queue.

And finally, if we want to use the mathematical average (or the mean), which is approximately 62% probability in our fictitious case (because I just said it was), then we have a lead time of 2 days, a throughput of 2.5 items per day, and our item should get done on the 6th day.

You'll notice, at no point are we negotiating over how long a specific item will take. If we need to adjust our tolerance, we change our probability target and run the math again.

# Silos

Most teams I work with have three distinct roles; BA, Developer, and QA. Most teams I work with have three distinct phases of their work; gather requirements, build, verify. Even on agile teams, these separations exist. There are clear delineations in the process and clear segregation of responsibilities. But this segregation is a contributor to erratic velocity. How many "agile" teams do you know of where the BA group is an iteration ahead of the developers who are an iteration ahead of QA, leaving us with a three-iteration cycle time and significant lag in our feedback loops between the groups?

Tighten the loops. Get people working together in not only close proximity, but close time-frame. Involve the developers and QA in the formation of requirements. Push QA to the front and automate, automate, automate. Don't let manual testing be a bottle neck. Start development before you've polished the requirements. And don't wait until the end to test it all comprehensively.

# Various Forms of Mismanagement

Herein lies my primary onus for the mantra, "Agile ain't practices". Agile is a set of values.

**Individuals and interactions** over processes and tools

**Working software** over comprehensive documentation

**Customer collaboration** over contract negotiation

**Responding to change** over following a plan

I see organization after organization pick up practices in the name of agile and apply them, devoid of the values. Most popular seems to be daily stand-ups and burn-down charts; two tools that provide project management with quick feedback on status so that they can make informed decisions about items such as task assignment or if the team needs to put in extra hours to make the deadline. (By the way, that sentence should make you cringe).

I knew a project manager (PMP) turned ScrumMaster (CSM). Actually, I've known many of these folks. And I don't mean to disparage them as a collective. This one, in particular, exhibited what I believe to be a common set of behaviors; They assigned the team tasks, asked for commitments, and chastised the team for failure to deliver to stretch goals.

Once, when the CSM was upset that the team had again failed to hit commitments, they said to the team, "If you can't start self-organizing to get it done, you can't have nice things."

I don't even know what that means; to have nice things. But it is clearly intended as a threat. There's some servant leadership protecting the team for you.

Assigning tasks, driving for excellence in estimating, pushing for points, treating code as if it is only a means to an end, role-based incentives, making the team's decisions for them, leaving the team to make all the decisions (they are self-organizing after all), splitting people's assignment across teams (they only need 1.5 QA), burdensome process, and failure to address impediments are but a few examples of mismanagement.

There are already numerous good books on the topic of managing software development teams, so I won't go into great detail here.

There are, however, a couple of things I do want to cover in a little more detail; individual incentives, and lack of autonomy.

## Individual Incentives

One of my all-time most popular tweets[25] states,

> "We simply ask that you be innovative without mistakes while working as a team toward individual performance goals."

Most folks readily scoff at, "be innovative without mistakes".

Innovation necessitates we do things that have never before been done. Innovation necessitates that we experiment and learn. Some (most) of those experiments are not going to validate our hypothesis. This, in some organizations, is considered a mistake.

Some of those experiments are going to have detrimental side effects, even if temporarily. This, in many organizations, is considered a mistake.

There is a clear tension between "be innovative" and "without mistakes". Asking folks to be innovative without mistakes is clearly ridiculous.

But the second half of this tweet, "working as a team toward individual performance goals," is no less ridiculous. We take a bunch of folks from various backgrounds with various specialties and we put them in a collective and ask them to work together. We expect them to collaborate, to be t-shaped, and to share the work.

We have them work together writing requirements. We have them work together writing code. They sit together in an open space.

[25]Norton, Doc. "We Simply Ask That You Be Innovative without Mistakes While Working as a Team to Achieve Individual Performance Goals." Twitter. Twitter, May 8, 2018. https://twitter.com/DocOnDev/status/993855609018769408.

They share ownership. They create shared plans. They set shared goals. They track progress as a team. They celebrate wins together.

Then, once per year, we advance them and give them raises based on how they did according to their personal goals and individual performance metrics.

If you are on this team and your manager gives you a personal goal of improving your React skills, but the majority of the work is in a Java codebase for which you are the only remaining original team member, you have to reconcile the tension between what's best for the team and what advances your career.

 A system that does not adequately take collaboration into account when reviewing it's members will not realize the full collaborative potential of those members.

If, as a part of personal performance reviews, management looks at the number of stories you delivered or commits you made, you are now disincentivized to mentor others, or possibly even pair. Each contribution you make that does not directly correlate to individual performance measures is a contribution that effectively counts against you.

This tension impedes a team from coming together. A system that does not adequately take collaboration into account when reviewing it's members will not realize the full collaborative potential of those members.

## Lack of Autonomy

Autonomy is the capacity to make an informed and uncoerced decision. As related to individuals at work, it means people have a high level of discretion in how they perform the work. When we speak of self-governing teams, we are speaking of autonomous teams; teams that hold the right to make their own decisions without being controlled by anyone else.

In agile software development, principles five and eleven speak directly to autonomy[26]:

 Build projects around motivated individuals. Give them the environment and support they need, and *trust them to get the job done.*

The best architectures, requirements, and designs emerge from *self-organizing* teams.

Organizations want the agile. It is good. They nod their heads when we say things like, "Self-governing teams", and, "Autonomous teams".

And then they put in centralized governance, controls, and approvals. They mandate that all teams use the same tracking software; ideally in the same way. They mandate standard reports which, in turn, require standard process. They mandate standard approved tools, languages, and frameworks. They require specific stage gates and checks, which by their very existence require teams to adhere to specific ways of working. A team writing automated acceptance criteria still has to have their use cases documented via the corporate template and approved before the official testing phase can begin, which must come after the development phase.

Hello? What?

This is not autonomy.

This is heteronomy: The subjection of a community to the rule of another power.[27]

---

[26]Principles behind the Agile Manifesto. Accessed January 26, 2018. https://agilemanifesto.org/principles.html.

[27]"Heteronomy." Heteronomy dictionary definition | heteronomy defined. Accessed January 26, 2020. https://www.yourdictionary.com/heteronomy.

There is benefit to having some standards. No doubt. But there is additionally benefit to eliminating any and all standards that fail to continue to serve the best interest of the organization. There is benefit to reducing policy from a strict set of steps to a set of fundamental guidelines.

Rather than mandate a process for how tests are written and executed, set a guideline that states all teams need to have and follow an approved testing strategy.

Rather than mandating iterations, velocity, and the like, set a guideline that states all teams need to manage the flow of work and be able to respond to change.

Create constraints that reduce options, but simultaneously empower the team. "No code can move into the master branch until three people have seen it.", is a simple enabling constraint. It is clear that no one person can write code alone and push it into master. But this constraint is also quite empowering. Teams get to decide for themselves how they'll do this. Maybe they mob so three or more people write all the code. Maybe they pair and ask for a review. Maybe they do formal code reviews. Maybe they use pull requests. Maybe they use combinations of all of the above.

## Big Agile and Autonomy

Welcome to Big Corp. We are excited to have you join us as a senior software engineer. You will be delighted to learn that we have adopted a scaled agile framework which allows us to run a very efficient agile organization.

As a member of a self-governing, autonomous, two-pizza sized, full-stack, devOps, self-contained, design to delivery squad, you will have the freedom and flexibility to execute on the work as you see fit within corporate approved standards.

Your team will be assigned tasks to execute with clear requirements written in Given/When/Then format. Here's an example task from our warehouse management team's backlog:

**Title:** Add receiving hours to dock.
**Promise Date:** In two weeks
**Description:**
In order to open and close the dock
As a receiving manager
I want to set receiving hours for a dock
**Details:**
Given I set receiving open for dock 3 to 6am
When it is 6am
Then dock 3 is open
[Many more details here]...

As you can see, we are following all the agile best practices for our tasks.

Now, tasks are always tied to stories. Your supervisor will work with the department integration team to define the stories. Stories are tied to Features, which help your supervisor know what is expected of the team. Managers, as members of the product steering team, are responsible for defining the features. Features are a breakdown of the Epics, which are defined by Directors. Those Epics are driven by Initiatives which the Vice Presidents design to support the Themes our Executives have laid out for the next 18 months.

Supervisors and Managers manage the dependencies across the squads.

*Ew.*

This is hierarchical oppression in autonomous agile clothing.

This task is almost entirely removed from the actual problem we are trying to solve. Sure, we are supposed to add receiving hours to a dock, but why? Because our dock configuration is missing receiving hours? That sounds like a lack of solution rather than an un-resolved issue.

This team is not likely to understand why they are doing what they are doing. They are essentially taking implementation orders and executing them. The company is losing out on an opportunity to leverage the creativity and knowledge of this team. By the time the people who do the work pick up an item, everything is detailed for them. Devoid of context and real understanding with a list of tasks to execute, the team has little to no real autonomy.

The business problems are opaque to the team. The team's creativity is stifled. And the company loses out on the team's knowledge and insights.

Let's take a look at this one task.

Why do we need receiving hours for a dock?
*So that we know when the dock is actively receiving.*

Why do we need to know when the dock is actively receiving?
*Because the nightly batch to update inventory needs to run after the dock closes.*

Why?
*Because the batch update is currently scheduled for 9pm and sometimes the docks are not done processing received inventory, which messes up numbers for the morning reports and throws off fulfillment calculations.*

How does knowing dock receiving hours solve this problem?
*If we know when the dock closes, we can figure out when to run the nightly batch.*

How would you do that?
*We will run batch one hour after dock closing.*

Does a dock always complete receipt processing within one hour from closing?
*Not if it was a busy day, they get backed up, or there is a large late shipment.*

So, don't we want to know when a dock has completed receipt processing rather than what their hours are?
*Umm... yeah...*

As it turns out, adding the ability to indicate a dock is done with receipt processing and notifying the nightly batch process is about one half day of work. This is assuming someone on the dock is willing to indicate when receipt processing is done by pressing a button on a screen. Whereas adding new fields to the database to record start and end, updating the maintenance screens, and configuring the down-stream processes to respect dock hours is a few weeks. Not only does the new solution actually solve the business problem in a more flexible and effective way, but it costs far less to build and maintain.

When we distance the team from the business, and the actual customers through layers of management, we lose out on many opportunities to discover even better solutions, such as the one detailed above.

In addition to all this, these layers of theme - initiative - epic - feature - story - task create another serious issue. The organization has reduced their ability to respond quickly to change. It takes weeks, if not months for information learned on the front lines at the task level to have an impact on the associated epics and then cascade back down to the tasks through features and stories. This is assuming the information ever makes its way to Directors.

Since the teams don't clearly know what business problem they are trying to solve, once a task is implemented, they need to scurry to the next one in order to meet the deadline. No need to look at data or confirm we've achieved the goal. We're done here. Task complete. Check.

Because critical business information isn't understood or gathered at the team level, there is the long delay in getting feedback from users to Directors through indirect means that don't involve the team. By the time Directors realize the need for a change and that change cascades down through the organization, teams have implemented a bunch of tasks that either need to be rolled back, significantly modified, or perhaps simply offer less value than the value that could have been realized.

Remove the layers of minutia. You probably don't need five work item layers. You maybe need two, possibly three. And do your best to always articulate the why of a story over the what. Help the team understand the business problem they are solving as well as they understand the proposed solution.

# Other Metrics

So I think we've made the case against Velocity as a metric. And we've given you some things to think about as you're considering what metrics to use instead (if any). Now let's take a look at some other metrics that might help you get to the root cause of team issues, help you figure out when things will actually be done, and help you figure out if you're doing a quality job - from a technical and customer perspective.

## Lead Time

In software development Lead Time is generally considered the time elapsed from the moment a request is received to the moment that same request is available in production. I call this the time from, "Hey, wouldn't it be nice if..?", to, "Hey, ain't that nice?"

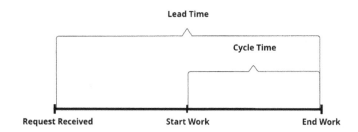

Lead and Cycle Time

For some teams, lead time is measured from when the team starts to look at the request. In these cases, the timer doesn't start when an item hits the backlog, but rather when the item gets picked up for analysis, or whatever is the initial step in the process. For our purposes, we are going to consider lead time to be from the moment a request is pulled from the backlog to be worked on. We're not going to concern ourselves with the amount of time an item sits in the backlog, as this has more to do with the volume of items and prioritization than it does with actual throughput and team capability.

Tracking the production lead time (time from work starting to in production) allows us to produce better projections for when an item will be complete. If we know there are seven items in the backlog ahead of this one with three items in progress for a total of 10 items ahead of this one and we know that on average an item takes 2 days from commencement to completion, we can reasonably estimate that this one will be done in 20 days. Sort of.

At first blush, an average seems perfectly reasonable for estimations. Essentially half of the items will complete sooner than the average and half of the items will complete later than the average with some amount falling precisely on the average. What we've just described here is a normal distribution, which when graphed results in what is often called a bell curve. With a normal distribution, if you use the average to estimate, you have a 50:50 shot of being right.

But you don't have a 50:50 shot of being right when you use the average lead time. Lead times don't happen on a perfect bell curve.

## Lead Time Distributions

Take a moment and think about a trip you take regularly. This might be your commute to or from work. Maybe it is visiting a family member.

For me, this is my commute to the client every day. For the past several months, I've been working with one primary client as we help them transition toward an experimentation mindset with a focus on flow and valuable outcomes.

I drive to the client from a nearby hotel. On average, that commute takes 10 minutes. Most mornings I catch at least one light or get behind someone doing 25 in a 40 for a mile or two. Some mornings, the lights are in my favor and the slow pokes stay out of my way. On such days, I can get from hotel to client in about 7.5 minutes. Under no legal circumstances can I get to the client faster than in seven minutes. Account for distance and general safety, and seven minutes is already pushing it; possible, but not likely. Under no physical circumstances can I get to the client faster than in five minutes. Even if I ignore all laws of man, the laws of physics still bind me.

On the other end of the spectrum, however, the commute can take (and has taken) much longer. For a couple of weeks, the main thoroughfare was under construction, reducing traffic to a single lane in the outbound direction on a road that is normally three lanes. One morning, there was an unusual amount of traffic and things got jammed up, causing everything to move quite slowly. People snuck out into intersections in hopes of slipping through before the light changed. Some didn't make it and the resulting jam caused people coming from perpendicular roads to do the same; stay in the intersection in hopes of making it through after things cleared. Basically, we were down to about two or three cars per direction clearing the intersection for every complete turn of the light.

I got stuck in a long line of traffic and with the other road closings and single lane restrictions, I had nowhere to go but forward. The light did a full rotation once every 6 minutes. There were approximately 15 cars in front of me. 27 minutes later, I cleared the light and finally arrived at the client a full 38 minutes after I'd left the hotel.

Let's imagine that I'd tracked my morning commute time to work each day and I recorded it on a sheet. And for the sake of this example, let's further imagine that my 38 minute outlier day had not yet occurred. That sheet might have looked something like this:

### Morning Commute

| Mon | Tue | Wed | Thu | Fri |
|-----|-----|-----|-----|-----|
| 10.25 | 9.5 | 9.75 | 10 | 12.25 |
| 10 | 15.25 | 12.5 | 10.75 | 9.25 |
| 10.25 | 10.25 | 9 | 10.5 | 10.25 |
| 10.5 | 10.75 | 13.75 | 11 | 11.25 |
| 14 | 12 | 10.5 | 13 | 10.25 |
| 11.25 | 13.5 | 11.5 | 14.25 | 10.25 |

The data shows us that while the trip can take no less then nine minutes, it can take as much as 15.25 minutes with an average trip time of 11.25 minutes. Our shortest trip is 2.25 minutes quicker than average. Whereas our longest trip is four minutes slower than average. And as we indicated, no matter how hard we try to get there sooner, we are ultimately bound by the laws of physics. But on the other end, in terms of how long the trip can take, we are pretty much bound only by the laws of reason.

Now, if you asked me how long it took me to get to work, I might say, "Between nine and fifteen minutes.", and I'd be accurate, but not precise. I could also say, "11.25 minutes on average," which is precise, but not necessarily accurate. But what if you were asking me to guarantee I could make it to work within the time I estimate? What if you were asking me to make a commitment and to guarantee with 100% certainty that I could get to work within the time committed? Does this sound familiar to you? Doesn't this sound like just about every "estimation" discussion you've ever had at work? Well, if this were the case, then based on the data available to me, I'd have to say, "I can get to work within 15.25 minutes."

A lot of people would say I am padding. But I am not padding. I am providing a 100% guarantee based on the data available. Which is what I was asked for.

Some would say I am gaming the system. More often that not, I make it to work in under 11 minutes. How could I possibly think an estimate of 15.25 minutes is reasonable? That's more than 25% padding on top of the average for something as simple as driving to work; same car, same driver, same route - every day.

But the reasonableness of my estimate is the wrong question, now isn't it? The right question is how could one possibly expect, in a system with such variability, that anyone could make a commitment they will be held accountable to and use a low probability number?

Low probability? What do I mean by a low probability number?

Well, let's look at the data again. This time, let's look at it on a distribution graph.

**Lead Time Distribution for Drive Time**

So far, so good. This is probably what you'd expect to see. A cluster of numbers near the low end with a peak around the average and a longer tail. This is a right-skewed distribution. Remember when we talked about how lead time doesn't happen on a perfect bell curve? For similar reasons to our commute, lead times for software development also happen on a right-skewed distribution. The term right-skewed indicates that the graph can trail off to the right for a significant distance. This is also referred to as a positively skewed distribution graph. In a distribution graph, our X axis represents increments increasing in value from left to right. So a tail that points right, points in the positive direction. Correspondingly a tail that points to the left, points in the negative direction.

Okay, so right-skewed distribution. Great. But what do I mean when I say a number is a low probability number? And why did I say the average was a low probability number?

Let's draw a line on the graph at the mean, or numerical average.

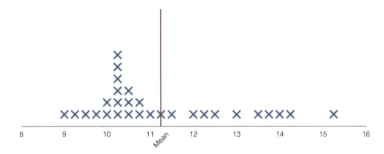

**Lead Time Distribution for Drive Time with Mean**

We can now see that 19 of the data points fall on or before the mean, while 11 of the data points fall after the mean. So if we were to use the mean (or average) as our commitment, the data tells us we have a 65.5% chance of hitting or bettering the commitment. That means we have a 34.5% chance of missing it. Or a one in three chance of going over our commitment.

So our probability for this estimate is roughly 66%. We expect to be over the estimate 33% of the time AND we expect to be under the estimate 62% of the time. We expect to actually hit the estimate, 3.4% of the time.

In most organizations, an estimate that we think we'll overshoot 33% of the time would be considered a low probability estimate. Certainly if there is gnashing of teeth when the estimate is missed, be it high or low, we're setting ourselves up for failure. If the repercussions for missing the estimate are significant enough, then the individual may determine it is in their best interest to fill any excess time when they finish "early" or cut corners when they think they might finish "late". And let's get this clear right now - those repercussions need not be drastic. The tedium of exploring why the estimate was wrong may be enough to encourage behavior that makes estimates look more "right".

I once worked with a team where the technical lead proudly announced that he was "excellent at estimating." He insisted that if others were as experienced and disciplined as he, they too could be excellent at estimating. Over time, he was able to come to realize that he was, in fact, excellent at hitting the estimates he'd made. These are not the same thing, but they present similarly on the surface; especially in an environment concerned with estimates over forecasts.

What we're getting at here is the usefulness of Lead Time Distributions. They are simple to create, easy to read, and give us an actual mathematical basis for forecasts versus the usual pseudomathy estimates found on many agile teams.

To create a lead time distribution, you chart the lead time of each story (or whatever you call a unit of work) on a simple graph. Along the X axis is time, most likely in days. The Y axis is the count of items that had a given lead time. The way I do it is usually a simple chart on graph paper with each square counting as a single unit. Say our first story completes with a lead time of 3 days. I place an X in the first box in my 3 column. The next story completes with a lead time of 5, so I place an X in the first box in my 5 column. The third story completes with a lead time of 3 and I place an X in the second square in my 3 column. At this point, my graph would look something like the following.

**Example Lead Time Distribution Graph**

The Lead Time Distribution graph then gives us a defensible way of running projections with probability intervals.

To finish this up, let's return to the example of my daily client commute.

I touched on probability earlier when we talked about using the average lead time for forecasting. You'll recall our probability for the average was roughly 66%. This is because, based on our data, we'll be at or under that estimate 66% of the time. If we want to increase our probability, we need to use a number that provides a greater chance of our hitting it or coming in under. If we want 100% probability, then we need to use 15.25 as that is the longest it has taken me to complete the commute. The following graph shows probability intervals of 50%, 75%, and 100% on the graph.

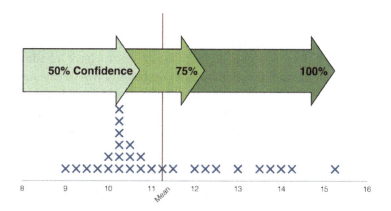

**Lead Time Distribution and Probability**

You'll notice that the higher the probability we want to have, the further from the mean we get and the distance does not increase linearly. The distance from 50% to 75% is almost half that from 75% to 100%.

Now what happens on that fateful day when construction delays are compounded by heavy traffic and bad morning attitudes, and I end up with a 38 minute commute?

**Lead Time Distribution after Bad Day**

Suddenly, we've got an outlier on our graph. What once looked like a spread of data points now looks like a cluster with one sole point way off to the right all by itself.

What to do?

We've a few options, I suppose. One, we could pretend it never happened; chalk it up to an outlier and forget about it. Don't graph it. Ignore it. Two, we could add it to the graph and have it haunt us forever. All future projections at 100% probability will be calculated at 38 minutes whereas a 95% probability would be calculated at 15.25 minutes. That seems a bit of a gap for 5% of probability, does it not? Or three, we could add it to the graph and make the graph rolling.

Our third option makes the most sense. Let's say there is some anomaly; an outlier that happens as a fluke or something that we can easily fix and it won't ever happen again. By rolling the lead time chart, that outlier doesn't haunt us forever. Also, by rolling the chart, our prior behavior has less weight than behavior that is more recent.

If a team is getting better at delivery, their throughput is going up, and their lead time is going down, doesn't it only make sense that their probability intervals would also tighten? By ensuring the Lead Time Distribution only looks back a reasonable time horizon, we ensure that the team is not over-influenced by activity long in the past over recent activity. I often have teams running one week increments with actual delivery at the end of each increment keep 16 weeks of data on a lead time distribution graph. If the team delivers less often, regardless of their iteration cycle, have them keep lead times for longer. You want sufficient data, say one hundred data points, to make sure you're getting a clear picture and your forecasts are well informed.

# Cycle Time

A common definition of Cycle Time is the time elapsed from the start of development to the beginning of testing. This is nearly correct, but definitely incomplete.

Cycle time is the amount of time for a work unit to move from one point to another point in a given process. It includes not only the time the item is being actively worked on, but also the time the item spends waiting to be worked on. The question, "What is your cycle time?" may prove impossible to accurately answer. Given cycle time is the measure of time for a work unit to move from one point to another, you cannot know the cycle time without knowing both points. It might be the time from when development picks it up to when formal validation commences. It might be from the time QA picks it up to when it is in production. And for any given project, there may be multiple cycle times; Design Cycle Time, Development Cycle Time, Testing Cycle Time, Deployment Cycle Time, Build Cycle Time, etc.

Cycle time is useful for evaluating specific pieces of your process. Teams with shorter cycle times are likely to have higher throughput, and teams with consistent cycle times across many issues are more predictable in delivering work. While cycle time is a primary metric for kanban teams, scrum teams can benefit from optimized cycle time as well.

Let's imagine a team that has a backlog from which they pull work into development. After development, they have a formal testing phase followed by formal business approval and deployment into production. There's a significant trade show coming up in a few months and we want to have some key features complete in time to reveal at the show. We suspect from our velocity that we won't get them all done on time.

In most organizations, we'd ask the team to move faster. But, what does that mean; to move faster? Can we work with less detailed requirements? Can we focus developers on coding and drop unit testing? Can we maybe hack a few things in?

The team cuts the corners and still doesn't hit the deadline. How is this? Their velocity, which was based on "development done", even went up.

Now let's imagine we've been tracking cycle times for each of our stages; development, testing, approval, and deployment.

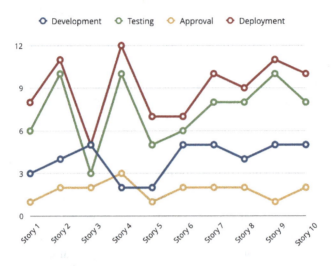

**Cycle Time By Stage**

It becomes obvious that Deployment and Testing take significantly longer on average than Development and Approval. Approval has the lowest cycle time whereas Deployment has the highest.

No matter how many corners we cut in development to speed things up, we're not going to see a significant improvement. Testing and deployment take much longer on average and both come after development. This means that even when development moves faster, their work builds up in a stack behind testing, which simply increases the average times for testing. Acceptance then responds relatively quickly, pushing a bunch of work into a wait queue for deployment, which may be able to increase their batch size, but will still take nearly twice as long as development. With cycle time data, we know materially which area (or areas) of the process needs to be our focus for improvement. Any effort to speed up processes prior to the bottleneck will fail to achieve faster delivery.

I've seen this scenario over and over again in organizations. A company puts in heavy process around testing and deployment in order to avoid mistakes which create significant bottlenecks, putting pressure on the teams to deliver faster, which increases errors through decreased rigor and quality, which justifies the need for even more process, and the viscous cycle continues.

Looking at cycle times, we can identify bottlenecks in the flow of work and focus our efforts on finding ways to improve processes that impact the bottleneck. Increase flow through the bottleneck and we increase flow through the entire system.

## Cycle-Time Control Charts

So we've taken a look at Cycle Time for the varying stages of our process and we've determined the issue is not necessarily with development. It appears there is more opportunity for improvement in testing and deployment.

Let's say testing, on average, takes slightly more than 12 days. We can take a look at all testing work and try to find ways to optimize it, but maybe there is a better way to look at the data.

A cycle time control chart can help us find outliers in our flow. By focusing in on these outliers, we can likely learn and improve more rapidly.

The cycle time control chart shows the cycle time for each story over a period of time. For each story that completes testing and moves into approval, we note the date it moved and the cycle time for testing.

Just like our lead times, cycle times occur on a right-skewed distribution. To be more specific, lead times and cycle times for agile software projects tend to fall on a Weibull distribution with a shape parameter between 1.3 and 1.6.

For a normal distribution, commonly referred to as a bell curve, we can apply standard deviation to help us focus in on the outliers. For a normal distribution, a single order standard deviation represents the 68.3rd percentile, a second order standard deviation represents the 95.4th percentile, and a third order represents the 99.7th percentile. Unfortunately, standard deviation does not apply correctly to skewed distributions. So we instead need to calculate a computed percentile[28].

A scatter diagram with lines for the 50th and 95.4th percentile gives us a basic cycle time control chart. The 50th percentile represents the median and the 95.4th percentile in this case approximates a second order standard deviation.

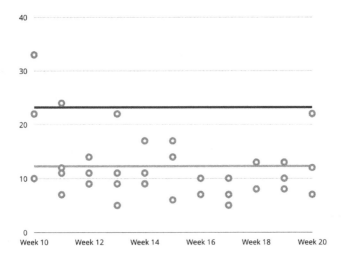

**Cycle Time Control for Testing**

We can see from our example chart, that the median cycle time in testing for these stories is 12.4 days, which is represented by the

[28]Magennis, Troy. "The Economic Impact of Software Development Process Choice Cycle Time Analysis and Monte Carlo Simulation Results." June 19, 2015. Accessed December 14, 2018. https://github.com/FocusedObjective/FocusedObjective.Resources/raw/master/Presentations/The-Economic-Impact-of-Software-Development-Process-Choice-Cycle-time-Analysis-and-Monte-Carlo-Simulation-Results.pdf.iÂ

gray bar. Our 95.4th percentile is at 23.2 days, which is represented by the red bar. While we want to drive the average cycle time down, it might be good to start with the outliers that are above the red bar. Not only do these push the average up, but they widen the "normal" range due to a larger deviation.

Focusing on those items above the red line, we can look for clues as to why they took so long, create a hypothesis about the cause, and devise an experiment to run. Maybe we determine that all of the high outliers involve a specific area of the code. Or perhaps they all involve the use of a specific technology or a specific workflow within the application. And, of course, there may be more than one reason for the issues. By focusing on the outliers, we narrow the possible causes and can be more confident that we are addressing the highest impact issues first.

Let's say all but one of these involve the use of data that takes 11 days on average to refresh from production. The team confers and determines that the data can be scheduled to refresh every 30 days and as long as the data has been updated in the last 90 days, it is sufficient for testing. The one significant outlier was due to testing of integration with a third party application. The team did not request a QA server for the application until the story was picked up for testing. They've added a simple check to their iteration planning meeting. For any stories that require integration testing, they now confirm a testing environment exists, and if not, make the request right away.

The next several weeks now look like the following graph:

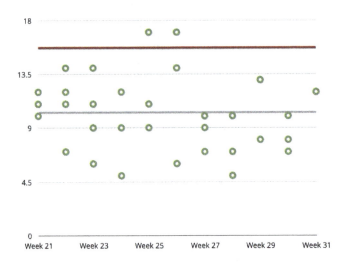

**Cycle Time Control for Testing after Optimizations**

The average (mean) cycle time in testing for these stories is 10.3 days and the 95.4th percentile has tightened from 23.2 days to 15.7 days, creating a new small set of outliers. The team can now focus in on these outliers, identify root causes, and start a new set of optimization experiments.

In addition to the outliers, you may want to pay some attention to trending and other indicators. We're not going to cover more detailed statistical process control in this book, but you may want to take a look at Nelson Rules[29] or Western Electric Rules[30] for identifying bias, trending, and noise. As an example, according to Nelson Rules, any time you have 14 or more points that oscillate above and below the mean, you have significant noise. This is something worth digging into even when none of the points are significant outliers. This much oscillation indicates a problem in the system.

---

[29]"Nelson Rules." Wikipedia. September 28, 2018. Accessed Jan 16, 2019. https://en.wikipedia.org/wiki/Nelson_rules.

[30]"Nelson Rules." Wikipedia. September 28, 2018. Accessed Jan 17, 2019. https://en.wikipedia.org/wiki/Nelson_rules.

# Cumulative Flow Diagrams

A Cumulative flow diagram (CFD) is a simple but very powerful tool used in queuing theory that helps to show the flow of work through a system. A CFD shows the quantity of work in a given state over time, which allows us to determine lead times, cycles times, Work in Progress, and changes in scope. I've often heard cumulative flow diagrams referred to as an alternative to the burn up chart, which is an alternative to the burn down chart. Just as email is an alternative to a printed letter which is an alternative to a hand written letter when I want to send the same urgent message to 50 people. All of them get the job done. One of them is so demonstrably better, the comparison suggests a strong penchant for less efficient tools, or suggests more than a bit of naivety.

## Making a CFD

To make a cumulative flow diagram is relatively easy. More and more agile tracking tools offer a CFD report so you might not need to generate your own. But, in case you ever do, let's walk through the basic steps.

Just about any spreadsheet software can be used to create a CFD. On a sheet, create a column for each step in your software process. The least you'd need would be To Do, Doing, and Done. I recommend a more detailed set of steps, especially for newer teams. Be honest about the steps most stories go through. If stories go through grooming before development, and there is a formal testing phase after development with a formal approval process to promote to production, I'd consider making columns for all of the action items as well as the wait states between the action items. We'll demonstrate this in a bit.

Each day, or at some other regular interval, total the work in each of the states you're tracking. I recommend once per day. If you do a daily stand-up meeting, the end of the meeting is a great time to run your totals as the board is going to be as accurate as it is going to be for that given day. Record the totals in the spreadsheet and create a stacked area graph against them.

For our example team, we're going to say they have a backlog from which they pull work into development. After development, they have a formal testing phase followed by formal business approval and deployment into production.

For this team, I'd create a sheet that looks like the following:

| Dates | Deployed | Approval | Testing | Development | Backlog |
|---|---|---|---|---|---|
| 3/6/17 | | | | | |
| 3/7/17 | | | | | |
| 3/8/17 | | | | | |
| 3/9/17 | | | | | |
| 3/10/17 | | | | | |
| 3/13/17 | | | | | |
| 3/14/17 | | | | | |
| 3/15/17 | | | | | |
| 3/16/17 | | | | | |
| 3/17/17 | | | | | |
| 3/20/17 | | | | | |
| 3/21/17 | | | | | |

Cumulative Flow Diagram Data - Empty

You might notice that the columns are in the opposite order of the actual flow of work. This is due to the way a stacked area graph works in most of the software I use. Your mileage may vary - it is a quick experiment to figure it out.

Then, as mentioned, fill in the values for each day (or whatever interval you select). Your stacked area graph will show the flow of work in a simple but useful way.

| Dates | Deployed | Approval | Testing | Development | Backlog |
|---|---|---|---|---|---|
| 3/6/17 | 0 | 0 | 0 | 0 | 22 |
| 3/7/17 | 0 | 0 | 0 | 2 | 20 |
| 3/8/17 | 0 | 2 | 2 | 1 | 17 |
| 3/9/17 | 2 | 2 | 1 | 2 | 15 |
| 3/10/17 | 4 | 2 | 2 | 1 | 13 |
| 3/13/17 | 7 | 2 | 1 | 2 | 10 |
| 3/14/17 | 8 | 2 | 2 | 2 | 8 |
| 3/15/17 | 12 | 1 | 1 | 3 | 5 |
| 3/16/17 | 13 | 2 | 3 | 2 | 2 |
| 3/17/17 | 18 | 1 | 1 | 2 | 0 |
| 3/20/17 | 20 | 1 | 1 | 0 | 0 |
| 3/21/17 | 22 | 0 | 0 | 0 | 0 |

Cumulative Flow Diagram Data - Populated

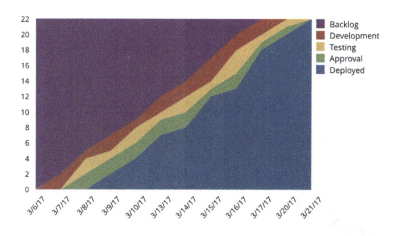

A Simple Cumulative Flow Diagram

# Reading a CFD

The above is a relatively simple cumulative flow diagram. The Y axis represents the amount of work in queue and the X axis represents time. Each color area on the chart represents a stage in the team's flow of work. Work starts in the form of stories in the ■ backlog. As the team works on a story, the major stages are ■

development, █ testing, and █ business approval. Once approved, they are deployed into █ production.

This first example is perhaps a diagram from a team in Lake Wobegon [31] where the scope never increases, there is no re-work, and everything flows through at a smooth even rate.

Thin relatively consistent lines moving steadily up and right with the backlog decreasing in size while the deployed to production increases in size are all signs of a team operating in healthy fashion. Healthy in this case, means delivering accepted work at a consistent (predictable) pace. A cumulative flow won't tell us everything. For example, it is possible that the code is of poor quality or that team morale is down. We wouldn't be able to determine either of these things by looking at the diagram. A cumulative flow diagram may not be able to help us see all possible issues, but it is good at helping us determine if our process itself is effective.

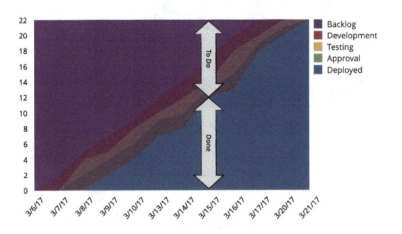

**To Do and Done**

First exposure to a CFD often leads to a sense of underwhelm. It looks like a multi-colored burn-up chart. And if we ignore the

[31]Lake Wobegon. (2017, April 15). Retrieved April 23, 2017, from https://en.wikipedia.org/wiki/Lake_Wobegon

stages that represent "doing", it is a burn-up chart. We can see the work to do and the work done. Add a simple trend line on the work completed and we've an actual burn-up, replete with an estimated completion date for the work remaining.

If this were all the value you got out of a CFD, it might not be worth the effort of tracking the data and generating the chart. But this isn't the only value one can get out of a CFD. Let's take a closer look and learn a bit more about how to read one.

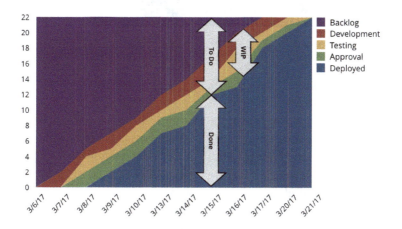

**Work In Process**

With a CFD, we can also see how much work is in process at any time including how much work is being attended to at each stage of the active process.

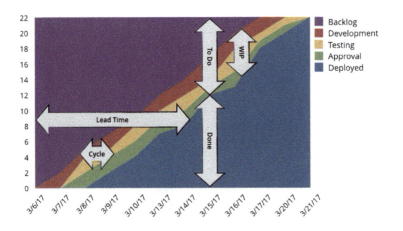

**Lead and Cycle Time**

We can also see the lead time and cycle time for stories, which gives us a clue about how long the overall process takes compared to the actual development effort. Adding more steps to the CFD, including times where items are waiting between activities can tell us a great deal about where the delays are in our process. This can help to focus our efforts for improvement. If it turns out that the most significant delay is when stories are waiting for testing, we can put more effort into looking at root cause and reducing the delays. Without this information, we might spend more time optimizing phases of work that increase the throughput prior to the bottleneck, which would produce no discernible improvement in delivery. Local optimizations done without understanding the system are a perfect path to increased waste without decreased lead time. A well thought out CFD can give us insight into the overall system.

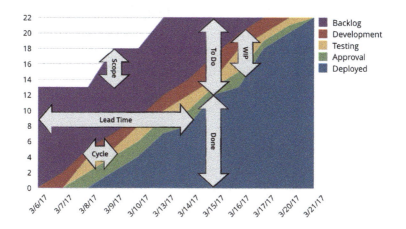

**Scope Change**

A CFD can also show us changes in scope. The above CFD shows two changes in scope for the project. In both cases, more work was added to the team. Changes in scope are represented through a raise (addition) or dip (removal) in the top line of the graph. Here we see that new work was added on March 7, pushing the delivery date from March 15 to March 17. And additional work was added on March 10, pushing the delivery date out to March 21.

## Getting Value out of a CFD

Alright. You can make a CFD and you can read a CFD. This is pretty good, but I want to help emphasize the benefit of a CFD.

Let's take a look at an imaginary team. This team has been together for multiple iterations, and their velocity is all over the place. The stakeholders are frustrated. New feature requests, even when expedited, take months to get into the customer's hands. This team is slow and unpredictable.

In a retrospective where they are discussing how they can improve their process, the team looks at a product burn down and a velocity chart. But can't determine a great deal from either.

What about you? Take a look at the Product Burn Down and the Velocity Chart below and see if you can make an educated guess about what challenges this team is facing.

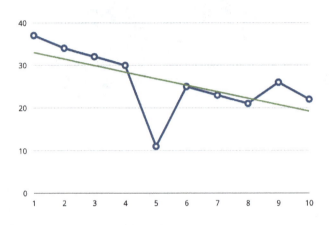

**Product Burn Down**

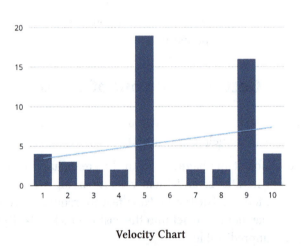

**Velocity Chart**

The team then takes a look at a Cumulative Flow Diagram for the same period of work and a key issue jumps out at them right away.

What about you? Take a look at the following CFD and see if you can make an educated guess about what challenges this team is facing.

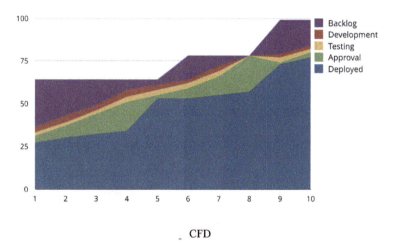

CFD

As you may have deduced, the team's primary challenge is in the approval process and delivery of new work. The product owner is a traveling sales person and does not have time for approvals when they are doing a lengthy tour of a foreign market. Upon their return, they review a bunch of features and then proceed to add new work to the backlog based on customer feedback they received while on the road.

A CFD tells us more about our process than most other charts and, as we've seen, it can often be fairly easy to intuit where the problems lie. If we discover that the development process is where the bottleneck seems to be, we have the options of breaking development down into smaller stages if appropriate, or perhaps looking at different types of work - such as stories versus fixes, or items that require database or infrastructure changes compared to items that don't to gain further insights.

# Delivery Frequency

 "If it hurts, do it more frequently, and bring the pain forward." — Jez Humble[32]

Delivery frequency is a measurement of how often we release software. When we combine it with things like escaped defects, we can see if releasing more or less frequently nets more or fewer defects.

In studies done on the impact of automated deployment processes and the use of version control for infrastructure management, Jez Humble and Gene Kim found "that high performing organizations ship code 30 times faster (and complete these deployments 8,000 times faster), have 50% fewer failed deployments, and restore service 12 times faster than their peers."[33]

The more frequently a team releases, the more truly efficient their processes need to be. Teams that release with high frequency have driven waste out of their environments in order to be able to do so. Formalized phases of integration and acceptance and regression testing are folded into the day to day process.

The rate of delivery is an indication of efficiency as the process needs to be optimized to safely deploy often. The rate of delivery is an indication of flexibility as it suggests the code changes are small and incremental.

While delivery frequency suggests these things, it does not guarantee them. I've seen many an environment where the team does minimal automated testing and takes pride in their ability to deliver

[32]"Continuous Delivery Quotes by Jez Humble." Goodreads. Goodreads. https://www.goodreads.com/work/quotes/13558958-continuous-delivery-reliable-software-releases-through-build-test-and.

[33]2014 State of DevOps Report. (n.d.). Retrieved June 29, 2017, from https://puppet.com/resources/whitepaper/2014-state-devops-report

often. I've seen numerous environments where delivery frequency includes patches and bug fixes. The teams are actually delivering new features at a slow pace, but are regularly putting out fires. I've had more than one release engineer explain the value of a fully automated deployment pipeline despite a lack of testing and other rigor; failing to realize how this might actually be contributing to the problem.

When looking at delivery frequency, consider it a team metric, not a departmental metric. What I mean by that is make sure to measure delivery frequency for each team. How often the department releases may not give a clear depiction of how teams are doing. A department of 3 teams may release 20 times per day on average. Look a little closer and you may find that one of the teams is releasing 19.7 times per day on average, one releases every day or two, and one has not released in several weeks.

Let's take a look at two departments, both of which are comprised of 10 teams and release 5 times per day.

### Department A

| Team | Releases Per Week |
| --- | --- |
| A | 2 |
| B | 3.25 |
| C | 2 |
| D | 3.5 |
| E | 2.25 |
| F | 3 |
| G | 2.25 |
| H | 2.25 |
| I | 2.5 |
| J | 2 |

Department B

| Team | Releases Per Week |
|------|-------------------|
| K | 1 |
| L | 2 |
| M | 1 |
| N | 5.25 |
| O | 2.25 |
| P | 7.25 |
| Q | 2.25 |
| R | 1.5 |
| S | 1.5 |
| T | 1 |

Both Departments release a total of 25 times per week on average. This might lead us to believe that teams are releasing 2.5 times per week and that the departments are similar in performance.

But if we look at the ranges for the values that comprise the mean, we see something telling. The range for Department A is 1.5, whereas the range for Department B is 6.25. For department A, no team is more than 1 release per week away from the average. For department B, some of the teams are off average by as many as 4.75 releases per week.

The average delivery is the same for both departments, but it turns out that department B has not only the highest performing teams, but also the lowest. If we looked at only the rate for the department, we wouldn't see this difference.

By including the range, we can identify departments with outliers and drill in to get more insight.

## Frequency of Features, not Patches

Make sure frequency of release is a measure of features, not patches. Certainly, the ability to deploy patches rapidly is a benefit, but it should not be the focus. The goal is for each team to be able to deliver actual value to the customer in the form of defect free features and functions.

Now, I am assuming support teams don't exist or that the support team is a triage team and the actual product team is responsible for break/fix. If, on the other hand, you are segmented into teams that write software and teams that fix broken software written by others, then the rate at which your break/fix team can deploy patches is a reasonable measure.

### Also, No Break/Fix Teams

I'm going to say this as straight as possible.

You shouldn't have a break/fix team.

If you have one (or many), restructure the teams so that the people that write the software are directly responsible for supporting it. Overall solution quality is reduced whenever you have some teams responsible for writing software and some teams responsible for fixing it.

By folding this responsibility back into the delivery teams, you allow them to learn more rapidly and encourage them to double-check requirements and quality. Break/fix teams encourage a lower quality product, and impede learning from happening where it is most valuable.

# Code Quality

Code Quality can be a contentious topic as the quality of the code is often subjective.

The business generally thinks the software is written with quality code so long as it performs the job at hand. This seems a reasonable measure. A piece of code that fails to serve a business need, no matter how well crafted, is not of any value.

The developer who originally wrote the code thinks the code is quality code because it both serves the business need and is written in the manner and style they personally chose. From indentation to variable names to the specific inner workings of each of the functions, the developer made hundreds if not thousands of decisions in the creation of this code. It is surely a quality job.

And along comes another developer. "This code is terrible," she claims. "It is convoluted and impossible to maintain." The original developer disagrees. He knows exactly where to go to add requested functionality. He can read the code no problem.

Is this good code or not? How do we assess quality?

Here's the thing. It is hard to assess quality from utility alone. If Bob, the electrician, wires your house poorly, but the finish on the house looks great, how do you know the electrician did a quality job? If you ask Bob, what is he going to tell you? If another electrician suggests some of the wiring should be re-done, Bob is going to tell you the other electrician is mistaken. Maybe the other electrician is just trying to scare you into spending money with them. I mean, you can plug stuff in and it works, right? All the outlets are in useful places. All the light switches work. All appears well. Then, one day, you come home from work to find the entire home in cinders from an electrical fire that started inside the walls.

This is why cities have building codes. It is hard to determine true quality by the look. In some cases, it is difficult to determine true quality by the use.

As a result, there is a standard by which all building construction is supposed to be done. There are independent inspectors who verify the work has been done to standard.

These standards are designed to protect us. They ensure buildings are constructed to a set standard. Without the standards and third party inspection, buildings were prone to all forms of issue. Lives were at stake. Collapsed roofs, flooding from burst pipes, fires from faulty electric systems.

In software, we've somehow convinced ourselves that this is not the case. That lives are not at stake. But software is everywhere. It is in your watch, your tv, your microwave, your car, and the trains in which millions of people commute each day. Software manages the traffic signals that operate throughout our cities, managing flow and keeping our cars from crashing into one another. Software supports the control of air traffic, keeping planes in the sky and at safe distances from one another. It is in the automatic doors entering the hospital, the heart rate monitor that checks your vitals, the pump that delivers your sedative, the systems that monitor your health during the surgery, and the dialysis machine that helped to keep you alive.

Even if lives were not at stake, which they most certainly are, software literally runs our economy. From accounting systems to online commerce to banking and the stock market itself, software runs every aspect of our world economy.

A building will impact the few who reside or work there. The largest office building in the world houses an order of magnitude fewer people than are driving at any given time, in the air at any given time, or in surgery at any given time. Software's potential impact is absolutely massive. And yet, the inspections in software are all around process, not construction.

For those companies subject to such regulation, software process is monitored and checked. Did the right people sign off? Was there a proper separation of responsibilities? Were high-level tests executed, and did they pass? Yet there are no checks for actual quality of construction.

If we equate software construction to electrical work, we might see the issue. Metaphorically, somebody is required to check that the switch was installed at the right time in the flow of work. Somebody is required to check that the switch works. Somebody is required to check that somebody checked the switch. There are audit trails to prove the switch was approved to be installed, that it was in fact installed, and that all switch checks were performed. But nobody is required to inspect the wiring. Ever.

We're going to look at ways to objectively inspect the wiring. The following are techniques we can use to quantifiably measure aspects of the code related to quality of construction. We'll look at metrics that either directly or indirectly quantify the quality of code.

## Escaped Defects

Escaped defects are defects in the system that managed to get into production. They've escaped the confines of the team and are now wreaking havoc in public.

An escaped defect is an indication of systemic failure. The systems we have in place for delivering software should prevent defects from getting into production.

Code is written in pairs, written in mobs, or reviewed via pull requests. It is possible you like to self-impose bottlenecks and prefer late feedback, so you're still using some formal code review meeting. But it is unlikely code moves without any form of peer review. Right?

 An escaped defect is an indication of systemic failure.

Unit and acceptance/regression tests are being written around the code you add or change. Developers are each running these tests dozens of times per day, if not more often. The continuous integration server runs these tests for every check-in, which is also multiple times per day. The team does a stop-drop-and-roll if the build is broken - including if tests fail. Right?

But what if the defect wasn't made here?

## Not All Defects Are Made at Home

The majority of people I talk to state that defect free code is impossible. I've read arguments about how the operating system and hardware controllers are not defect free, therefor anything written on top of them will also have defects.

I've experienced the reality of bugs in the operating system impacting our software. I had a client that asked us to write a system that routed forms to varying printer locations based on where the recipient was located within the building. This was for a medical center prior to smart phones, and they wanted to get paperwork and messages to doctors as fast as possible. So we wrote a system that integrated with both the scheduling system and the keycard security system to determine where doctors were at any given time. Messages targeted for the doctor would then route to the nearest printer and be placed in pickup bins for internal couriers to deliver.

The night before we went live, the company's Tech Department rolled out an update to Microsoft Windows. The launch was less than spectacular. The first message was keyed in, minutes went by, but no report on the printer. "You need to fix this," the client told me.

We ran a print job from Microsoft Word. No problem. Then we ran a report in the medical records system. No job on the printer.

"It appears to be an issue with the printer drivers," we told the client.

"Nope," they responded, "Everything was fine until you installed your software."

We ran another medical systems report from a system that didn't have our software installed on it. No job on the printer.

"It is not our software," we said.

"Not our problem. You were hired to write software that works. Your software doesn't work. We won't pay you the remaining balance."

So we looked deeper and it turned out that the Windows update was rolled out with a misconfigured initialization file for Windows, including improper printer settings. Any piece of software that relied on the Operating System for printing would fail. Microsoft Office products, at that time, worked off of their own configurations. We updated the printer configurations, showed their team what we'd done and rolled out the updates. Take two - the jobs routed and everyone was happy.

For a while.

Three weeks later, we got another call from the customer. Some messages were not making it to the target printer. Would we please come in and take a look. That is, if we want to get paid.

This time, it was a little more difficult to figure out. After some research and testing, we determined that the issue was a flaw in the Novell network operating system. Approximately one print job in every 100,000 would report success, but never actually print. Our application was working fine. Windows was working fine. The network operating system was broken and reporting false positives.

We delivered the analysis and links to the Novell documentation showing the patch would be in an upcoming release of their operating system. Of course, the medical center was intentionally behind on releases, so they wouldn't see the patch for at least another twelve months.

"Fix it," was the word from the client.

So, much to our dismay, we added a confirmation feature to the software. For each job, a print confirmation was routed to a workstation near the printer. Now, before the job was placed in the pick-up box, someone had to acknowledge receipt. For any given job, if the job prior and after were both acknowledged, we sent it again.

Fixed. I guess.

## But Most Defects Are Made at Home

While there are examples that support the argument that you can't have defect free code due to issues in the operating system and controllers, it doesn't justify a lack of effort. By this same logic, if a framer suspects the foundation was poured under less than ideal conditions, then they might as well ignore building code because the home is already flawed in a way that might impact the owner.

The framer has a professional responsibility. If they feel the foundation is too weak to build on top of, they need to raise the concern. Or to even refuse to build on top of it. If they feel the foundation is slightly flawed, but not critically so, then they have a professional responsibility to frame well; to the best of their ability - or at least to code.

Such is the same for the software developer. We've a professional responsibility to do our jobs to the best of our ability.

Most of the defects in today's software are not a result of the operating system or hardware drivers. Most of the defects in today's software were put there by us.

We write clever solutions to complex problems. We stick with our first implementation because it is "done" even though we now know of a better solution. We leave a few smells[34] in the code because it works and that's all that matters. We form teams around technical skills instead of around products or business need, because our managers know more about the technology than they do about management or leadership. Over time, these compromises and mistakes add up and strange defects start to appear in production.

---

[34]Code Smell. Accessed March 24, 2018. http://c2.com/xp/CodeSmell.html.

## Remember The Goal is to *Release* Defect Free Software

Writing defect-free code is practically impossible. But releasing defect-free code is definitely possible.

Each developer has a local environment where they can run a comprehensive set of automated tests to verify the interactions and behavior of the code. Developers write tests along with the code, validating new behavior as they go along. Developers merge in other code changes and test yet again before pushing to the code repository. The continuous integration server runs all tests and flags the push as bad if even one test fails. Developers check each others code before accepting the pushed changes that just passed all of the tests. The code is deployed to another server where the entire automated test suite is run again to validate that everything works in a non-development environment. Humans perform exploratory testing. We run tests for load to make sure the code can hold up to the demand in production. In many organizations, the code is checked yet again in a near-production environment.

 Writing defect-free code is practically impossible. But releasing defect-free code is definitely possible.

If a defect is discovered at any point along this path then the code changes are rejected, and the development team makes the necessary changes. The cycle repeats until we find zero defects. Then, it goes to production.

In many organizations, if there is an outage due to a defect in code production, then an analysis of the root cause takes place in order to learn and make sure that the situation doesn't repeat itself. What if we did a light-weight version of the analysis when a defect showed up in staging? Or even in the integration environment? What if learning were important at every stage of the cycle, not only when a customer was affected?

Releasing defect-free code is definitely possible. I've seen it done in environments far less rigorous than the one I just described.

In measuring escaped defects (defects that make it into production) what we are looking for is primarily the rate at which defects escape and secondarily the number of defects at large. It is helpful to know how many defects exist in production at any given moment. If you find yourself in a situation where you are classifying defects such that some are deemed not important enough to fix, I suspect you are in serious trouble. Classifications for defects tend to get introduced once the defect escape rate is high enough that we feel like we can't keep up.

I encourage you to pay attention to the rate of escape. How many defects per time period are you experiencing? This is a number that is ideally on the decline, but certainly not increasing. How does the rate of escaped defects compare to the rate of story delivery? Ideally, the rate of delivery is steady or increasing while the rate of escaped defects is in decline.

I suggest you measure both escaped defects and delivered stories. Divide the number of escaped defects in a time period by the number of stories delivered in that same time period to get a ratio that can be used over time. For example, if you delivered 84 stories in a month with 3 escaped defects, then your escaped defect percent is 3.57% It's never good if the number of escaped defects per month increases. But looking at the ratio can help you determine of the overall quality of the code is in an accelerated decline or not. Say a year later, your escaped defects is now up to 5 per month. This is not good. But if your rate of story delivery is now 147 per month, your percent is down to 3.40%. While not a huge drop, it is a relief to know that while you are delivering more stories, your ratio of defects has actually decreased slightly.

# Code Complexity

## Cyclomatic Comlexity

Cyclomatic complexity[35], also known as the McCabe number, is a quantitative measure of the number of linearly independent paths through a program's source code. It is basically a count of the decision paths through the code. A piece of code with no if statements or conditionals has a cyclomatic complexity of 1. A piece of code with a single if statement that behaves differently based on whether the statement evaluates to true or to false has a cyclomatic complexity of 2.

Based on a graph analysis of the code, this metric was originally intended as a way of determining the minimal number of tests required for a piece of code. If the code has a cyclomatic complexity of 3, then it would require a minimum of 3 tests to exercise 100% of the code. This is assuming, of course, that the tests were written quite specifically to test each logical branch in the code.

In the original 1976 paper on the metric, McCabe notes that there appears to be a correlation between the complexity rank of a piece of code and the project members anecdotal assessment of reliability for the same code. Since then, a direct positive correlation between cyclomatic complexity and escaped defects has been determined. The higher the complexity, the more escaped defects. We cannot say that a cyclomatic complexity of 27 will net 8 bugs, or that a specific method with a low cyclomatic complexity will never have a high incidence of escaped defects. What we can say is that overall, statistically, the higher the complexity, the more bugs exist.

As a general rule, keep methods to a cyclomatic complexity measure under 7.

---

[35]McCabe, T. J. (1976, December). A Complexity Measure. Retrieved April 13, 2017, from http://www.literateprogramming.com/mccabe.pdf

# ABC Score

An ABC Score[36] is a score based on *Assignments* - where a value is assigned to or transferred into a variable, *Branches* - where a piece of code calls any other piece of code, and *Conditionals* - similar to cyclomatic complexity, this is a count of conditional statements (if, case, switch, etc.) in the code.

An ABC Score was devised as a size metric, not as a quality metric. The size metric was intended to be used, among other things, as a way to forecast the completion of a project. To calculate an ABC Score, we sum these three orthogonal aspects of the code and represent them as a 3-D vector < Assignments (A), Branches (B), Conditionals (C) >. It can also be represented as a scalar metric which is the magnitude of the vector < Assignments (A), Branches (B), Conditionals (C) > and is calculated as follows:

```
1    |ABC| = sqrt((A*A)+(B*B)+(C*C))
```

The original theory was that we could take the scalar metric of the code generated in a single day of development, divide it into the estimated scalar metric of the entire application and get the number of days required to complete the code base.

So if we estimate that an entire code base will require 300 assignments, 250 Branches, and 180 Conditionals, then we can represent the ABC Score for the entire code base as <300, 250, 180> or 430. If on a given day we write code that contains 10 assignments, 2 branches, and 8 conditionals, we can represent that as <10, 2, 8> or 13. Theoretically, we can then divide the ABC score for the single day into the ABC score for the application and get the number of days to complete the entire application.

---

[36]ABC score. (2017, March 11). Retrieved April 12, 2017, from https://en.wikipedia.org/wiki/ABC_score

```
1   <300, 250, 180>
2   sqrt((300^2)+(250^2)+(180^2)) = 430
3
4   <10, 2, 8>
5   sqrt((10^2)+(2^2)+(8^2)) = 13
6
7   430 / 13 = 33
```

This technique was not widely adopted. I assume, in part, because if we knew enough about the code we were going to write to get a count of Assignments, Branches, and Conditionals, we'd know enough to use better forecasting techniques. The truth is, we usually don't know these details until after the fact.

One distinct drawback to an ABC Score is that the calculation necessarily varies from language to language because of the differences in how languages implement different constructs.

One advantage is that an ABC Score is independent of any coding style and is therefore a more objective measure than measures such as lines of code or even Cyclomatic Complexity.

While not a quality metric, there is a direct positive correlation between an ABC Score and the number of bugs in an application.

Today, most people consider ABC to be a complexity metric and therefore use it as an indicator of quality.

## Lines of Code

*WHAT!?!*

Am I honestly advocating for lines of code as a code quality metric? Didn't we learn this was wrong in the 1970s?

I am advocating for it. Because we failed to learn an important lesson.

 More code doesn't make for a healthier solution.

It was once common in the industry to measure a developer's productivity by their "output". If we think that the role of developers is to write code, then we probably think that code is their output. If code is the output of a developer, then the more code they write in a given time frame, the more efficient they are. This is logical.

It is also, as it turns out, wrong. You see, developers solve problems and create solutions through code, much like surgeons cure ills and provide remedies through surgery. And just as more surgery doesn't make for a healthier patient, more code doesn't make for a healthier solution.

When developers were evaluated for their output, solutions became verbose.

Let's imagine a solution for calculating a relatively simple sales tax of 6%. Our company has a single store in Summit County, Ohio and sells taxable products. Calculation of sales tax is simple:

**Simple Tax**

```
1  def grand_total items
2    total = 0
3    items.each do |item|
4      total = total + item.price * 0.06
5    end
6    return total
7  end
```

Time goes by, and our store is now in multiple counties. Each county has a unique tax rate and some counties have an additional tax on certain types of items, such as cigarettes or alcohol.

**Multiple Tax Rates**

```ruby
def grand_total items, county

  total = 0

  items.each do |item|
    if county.name == "Medina"
      if item.type == "cigarettes"
        tax_price = item.price * 0.125
        total = total + tax_price
      else
        tax_price = item.price * 0.07
        total = total + tax_price
      end
    else
      if county.name == "Jackson"
        if item.type == "alcohol"
          tax_price = item.price * 0.11
          total = total + tax_price
        else
          tax_price = item.price * 0.09
          total = total + tax_price
        end
      else
        tax_price = item.price * 0.06
        total = total + tax_price
      end
    end
  end

  return total
end
```

You might be thinking to yourself, "That's not too bad." But I've personally seen places where this kind of thing got way out of hand.

Add in a few more counties, different taxes on different specialty items all in the same county, and you've got a very long mess of code. Now, we change the item.price to item.base_price and there are hundreds of lines of code to change and test. What if we missed one?

Could we write this in a way that wasn't so verbose?

**Multiple Tax Rates Cleaner**

```
1   def grand_total items, county
2     total = 0
3     items.each do |item|
4       total += item.price + (item.price * determine_tax(cou\
5   nty, item.type))
6     end
7     return total
8   end
9
10  def determine_tax county, item_type
11    tax_table = {
12        "Medina": {"cigarettes": 0.125, "standard": 0.07},
13        "Jackson": {"alcohol": 0.11, "standard": 0.09},
14        "Summit": {"standard": 0.06},
15        "": {"standard": 0.0}
16    }
17
18    return tax_table[county][item_type] || tax_table[county\
19  ]["standard"]
20
21  end
```

There are actually numerous advantages to this approach. The most significant of which is that we can now add a new county with standard and specialty tax rates by adding a single line of code. We'd simply add another entry to the tax_table. What was previously a copy, paste, and modification (or what I frequently refer to as copy, paste, molest) of multiple lines of code - resulting in a longer, harder to read, harder to maintain code base that was more prone to bugs - is now a single line entry with no logic changes. And if we wanted to, we could push the tax rate data to a database where someone in operations could update it and we'd have no need to deploy additional code.

Non-developers might argue that the former version was more readable. It was laid out just like we think about the problem, so it would be easier to follow. But the latter version is actually more readable to a developer. It takes a developer much less time to figure out what the short code is doing and to feel confident that it doesn't have strange typos or bugs.

But is fewer lines of code always better? Well, no. Using various techniques, it is possible to condense three or four lines of easy to read code down to a single convoluted line. We can collapse logic into complex statements that are difficult for a human to parse.

That said, statistically, fewer lines of code is better. Code Climate[37] is a code analysis tool that evaluates code based on numerous metrics, and provides developers a report card on the quality of the code. The folks over at Code Climate run analysis against hundreds of thousands of lines of code every day. In this effort, they've learned a number of things about code in general and about code quality metrics. For quite a while, they debated over Cyclomatic versus ABC complexity.

In the end, they discovered that the two were fundamentally the same in their correlation to bugs within the code overall. The higher the complexity, whether Cyclomatic or ABC, the more bugs that exist in the code. What surprised them a bit, however, was to discover that lines of code was equally as telling. Cyclomatic complexity, ABC complexity, and lines of code are all positively correlated.

---

[37]https://codeclimate.com/

More lines of code means more bugs. Fewer lines of code means fewer bugs.

And this is why I recommend lines of code as a quality metric. The more lines of code you have, the more bugs you have.

## Test Coverage

Test Coverage isn't really a measure of quality. Test coverage is nothing but a measure of how much of the code is covered by tests. I've seen plenty of teams with high test coverage achieved through some form of integration test with awful internal code quality. I've seen teams with extremely low coverage with good, if not excellent, internal code quality.

So why would I advocate for test coverage as a metric and why would I further classify it as a quality metric? I mean, I just said it isn't really a measure of quality. That's true. Test coverage is not a measure of quality, but having test coverage is an indicator of quality.

Allow me to explain. Code that is poorly written is hard to test in isolation. And code that is hard to test in isolation is poorly written. To test in isolation is to test a single piece of functionality, such as a method or function, without exercising code in other methods or functions. The more dependencies the code has, the more complex it is, and the more convoluted the internals, then the harder it is to test in isolation. The inverse is also true; the easier code is to test in isolation, then the less convoluted it is, the more simple it is, and the fewer dependencies it has.

 Test coverage is not a measure of quality, but having test coverage is an indicator of quality.

If I cannot test a method without also testing another method, then the two methods are said to be coupled together. When methods are coupled together such that I cannot test one method without testing both methods, then there is a good chance I cannot change the first method without changing both methods.

If we find this kind of coupling once or twice in a code base, it might be of little concern. But the more often it happens, the harder it is to extend or update the code. The application gets brittle; seemingly trivial changes have cascading impact. One small change can break several things, some of which seem un-related. Corrections to those breakages result in yet more cascades.

The more often a "simple" change takes far longer than one might expect, the higher the chances are you have a poorly constructed code base.

Unit tests, tests that validate a method's behavior without calling any other methods, are only possible when the code is constructed in a way that indicates loose dependencies or loose coupling. The amount of code successfully covered by unit tests, therefore, is an indication of how well the code is written.

## Don't Set a Target

A common mistake I see is teams who get excited about test coverage and set a goal for it. Once they can see how test coverage negatively correlates to bugs and cycle times, they want more coverage in order to reduce defects and to deliver faster. The logic is usually that if 30% test coverage is good, then 50% must be better and 100% would be better still.

Don't do this.

100% coverage indicates tests over all possible forks and branches of the code. It suggests that all edge cases and exceptions have been tested. While this sounds good in theory, when we make coverage the goal rather than good testing the goal (which is harder to quantify), we might miss defects even though we hit our target coverage number.

That's right; 100% coverage doesn't mean you'll find all the bugs.

Let's take a look at a simple piece of code with two if statements in it.

**Less Than Four**

```
1   # Always return a number less than 4
2   def less_than_four(first_check, second_check)
3     result = 0
4     if first_check
5       result+=1
6     else
7       result+=2
8     end
9
10    if second_check
11      result+=2
12    else
13      result+=1
14    end
15
16    return result
17  end
```

Now, we cover this code with a couple of tests which exercise both the "if" and the "else" for each of the checks.

**Tests**

```
1   expect(less_than_four(true,true)).to be < 4
2   expect(less_than_four(false,false)).to be < 4
```

This gets us to 100% test coverage. But in this case, 100% coverage is not enough. A test for (false, true), returns a result equal to 4, which is a bug per the intended behavior of the function. 100% coverage means we've passed through each line of code at least once in our testing, it does not mean we've exercised all combinations and permutations of the code.

You might be thinking, "Okay, Doc. But isn't that an argument for 100% test coverage as a minimum target?"

Perhaps. In this case, I am saying 100% test coverage isn't sufficient enough to indicate we're bug free. I am saying that our test coverage needs to be thought through, not just based on a minimum target.

In some cases, like the one described above, 100% test coverage is simply not enough. And in some cases, 100% test coverage is simply too much.

Let's take a common scenario where a team is working on a long-established code base. The product has been around for three or four years, consists of hundreds of thousands of lines of code, and has no automated tests to speak of. I see this in a great number of organizations that rely on manual testing, or organizations that tried to use some form of record/playback test automation until it got too hard to maintain and abandoned the effort. In either case, they've now got 0% test coverage.

What is this team to do? Do they try to get all the code covered with tests? If so, do they stop feature development until they have 100% coverage? Or maybe they set a target of 100% and try to both deliver new features and increase coverage.

I say they do none of these things. Instead, concentrate on writing tests around the code you're working in. Don't bother with anything else. If you need to change existing code, write enough tests to feel safe making the change. If you are writing new features or functions, get comprehensive testing around them. Make sure anything you modify or add is well tested. Don't worry about the rest. Code that has been in production, has no existing tests, has no reported defects, and doesn't need to change doesn't need test coverage at the moment. When there is a defect reported, or the functionality needs to change, then you need tests around it.

Following this technique, you are addressing the highest risk - the code with the highest churn rate. The term churn indicates the rate of change. Code that changes often is said to have a higher churn rate than code that changes infrequently or not at all. It may turn out that numbers as low as 30% overall test coverage are sufficient to safely work on the code base and help to ensure no new escaped defects. Focusing on 100% coverage for the entire code base would result in a lot of work with very little return. In these cases - and my experience is that these are the common cases - 100% could reasonably be considered too much test coverage.

So if 100% test coverage may be insufficient and 100% test coverage may be too much, you can see why I don't advocate for test coverage targets. No single number universally indicates quality or safety. Test coverage needs to be achieved intentionally; thinking about what needs to be tested, and why and how.

If we don't set a target, why have the metric at all?

Interesting question. While no one number is a clear indication of sufficient or insufficient test coverage, test coverage is negatively correlated to risk. An increasing percentage of test coverage indicates a diminishing risk, a decreasing percentage of test coverage indicates a growing risk, and a steady percentage of test coverage indicates a steady level of risk. This is a generalization. You can't count on test coverage alone as an assessment of risk. Test coverage won't tell you about the market, how brilliant your idea is, or whether or not you've sufficient funds to keep operating. But, in monitoring the trend of test coverage around the code with high churn, you can get a sense of risk around changes to the code base.

 Test coverage needs to be achieved intentionally; thinking about what needs to be tested, and why and how.

# Code Churn

Code churn indicates the amount of change that takes place in a particular area of code.

It is not actually a measure of code quality. But it is an important partner to other code quality metrics.

Code churn tells us where we are spending the most time in the code, making updates, adding features, fixing defects. The higher the churn, the more time the team spends in that area of the code. The more time spent in an area of code, the more risk there is if the code is low quality or doesn't have good coverage.

If we have a product that has two particularly snarly areas of the code, both with high complexity and low test coverage, which one should we fix first? The one with the higher churn.

Lower churn code is lower risk to the organization.

In fact, churn is so significant, a piece of code with no coverage, sky-high complexity, and any other number of internal issues that happens to work and has zero churn is a piece of code we can safely leave alone until absolutely necessary. Absolutely necessary being when business requirements indicate we need to make changes to it.

While I encourage teams to look at churn and use it to help them make decisions about what areas of the code to clean, there is a much more simple heuristic to use.

## Clean the Code You Are In

As mentioned, churn indicates where you spend the most time in the code. If you spend a lot of time in an area of the code, it is wise to clean it up. So, as it works out, if you are in an area of the code, then it makes sense to clean it up a bit. If, every time you are in the code, you clean it a little, the areas of the code where you spend the most time will get cleaned the most. The end result is the same as if you'd used churn as a guide, except you wouldn't have to measure churn and the code would already be cleaned (at least a little).

This technique of cleaning the code you are in is often referred to as "The boy scout rule". One of the "rules" of scouts is to leave the campsite better than you found it. In this metaphor, the campsite is our code. Leave the code better than you found it. Implement the feature, fix the bug, do whatever it is the story indicates you're supposed to do. And while you're at it, rename a variable, extract a method, or make any other small simple change that improves the readability, maintainability, and quality of the code. If everyone on the team does this, the code that gets touched the most will be in the best shape.

# Team Joy

A few years ago, I was working with a client who had started an initiative around joy at work. They'd devised a short survey which was sent to employees on regular intervals with the intent of measuring their levels of joy and engagement. The response rate was relatively low company wide, but it was abysmal in software engineering. From feeling disrupted, to thinking the questions were not relevant to work, to a sense that nobody was doing anything with the data anyway, there were numerous reasons given for why people weren't responding to the surveys.

Most of the metrics we were gathering from the software teams were relatively passive. They were measures of the flow of work, such as lead time and cycle time, or measures of the output itself through static analysis. Basically, developers went about their normal day and measures were taken without any disruption to their normal routines. Our team joy measures were, however, a disruption. They didn't fit into the flow of a normal day.

We thought we might be able to get an increase in participation if we figured out a way to work the survey into their flow of work. I'd seen this already with things like time tracking where we used a piece of software that kicked off automated tests every time a file was saved to also update a time log. Developers then used that log data to help them fill out timesheets.

But what to do for measuring employee joy in a passive way? After some discussion, we decided to try something very simple. All of the software source code was managed in a version control system known as git. The idea behind git and other version control software is to allow developers to manage changes to shared source code on a team; to control what changes are approved and make it into a final version, and to be able to revert the code easily to a prior working version if something goes wrong. Every time a developer submits a change to the source code they issue a commit command, which checks it into the source code management tool for consideration as a formal change. Every commit includes some note to indicate what the change is for, be it adding a new feature or fixing a defect.

Git, the source code management tool, is a piece of software written for developers by developers. As such, it has a relatively simple way of adding new functionality to it. We updated it so that it could interpret the messages developers included in every commit. For these teams, they already had a policy of including a work order number at the start of every commit message. This made it easy to track the change request the work was related to. A typical commit message looked something like:

```
1   AAA12345 - Corrects tax calculation for food items.
```

The first bit before the hyphen is the work order number. The rest is a quick description of the work itself.

We simply changed the format of the message to include a number from 0 to 5 which represented the developers opinion of the code using the following guidelines:

0 - Terrible quality
1 - Very Poor quality
2 - Poor quality
3 - Good quality
4 - Very Good quality
5 - Excellent quality

The same commit message might now look like this:

```
1   AAA12345 - 4 - Corrects tax calculation for food items.
```

In this commit message, we can see that the developer found the code to be good quality and was probably relatively easy to work in, but didn't feel it was the highest quality the team was capable of.

Our theory was that, given developers spend their days writing code, their opinion of the code itself might serve as a proxy for their joy or satisfaction at work. Spend many days in code you think is hard to read and breaks too easily, and you are probably not enjoying the work all that much. The code itself gets in the way and impedes you from working on the problem at hand. Conversely, if the majority of your time as a developer is spent in code that is easy to read and change, you are better able to focus on solving the problem at hand, and are likely to enjoy the work more.

Comparing commit scores with data from one on one meetings, we saw a positive correlation between the scores and employees expressions of joy or frustration with their work. Over time, we saw correlations between scores and employee mobility or exit rates. And quite valuably, we saw developer joy as a bit of a leading indicator. If joy scores were trending down, within a few weeks we almost always saw an increase in escaped defects, a hit to throughput, or some other indication of challenges on the team. If joy took a dip, it was best to talk about it in retrospective and see if we could get to the root cause. In a lot of cases, explicitly making the clean up of the code in question a work item not only improved joy, but it improved many code quality metrics.

An example of the git hooks used can be found on my public GitHub page: https://github.com/DocOnDev/team_joy

# Forecasting

"How long is it going to take?"

We get asked this question often. So very often. And the truth is, hardly anybody wants to really know how long a story or feature is going to take. What they want to know is when it will be done. And perhaps, more accurately, they want to know when they can have it or perhaps when they will be able to get the value it promises.

The most common technique I see for forecasting is good old velocity math. Add up the work required to deliver the feature and divide it by the team's velocity. This gives you the number of iterations it will take to deliver the feature. Now multiply the number of iterations by the iteration length to determine how long it will take.

Let's say, for example, that our velocity for the last three iterations is 8, 16, and 15, for an average of 13. Each iteration is two weeks. Let's say the feature we are targeting is 84 points and there are an additional 24 points worth of work prioritized higher than some of the stories that comprise the feature. In other words, in order to deliver the feature, we need to complete a total of 108 points, even though the feature itself is only 84 points.

```
1   108 / 13 = 8.3 (round to 9)
2   2 * 9 = 18
```

According to our typical "forecasting" technique, this work will be done in 18 weeks.

Cool.

How probable is this forecast? As we discussed in the section on Lead Time Distributions, the probability of the typical velocity math is pretty low - somewhere in the 50% range. A coin toss, more or less.

Given enough lead time data, we could use the lead time distribution to help with forecasting, but there is an even better way.

Fortunately for us, Troy Magennis and the team at Focused Objective have done a great deal of work in this area and provide us a simple tool that allows us to forecast[38] using a Monte Carlo simulation to produce a probability distribution.

That's a mouthful.

Essentially, their forecaster takes some basic inputs, such as throughput history, amount of work remaining, and average story split rate[39] and it runs 500 simulations to calculate the probability of the work being completed by a date. The simulations are run by randomly selecting from the variables provided. For each of the 500 simulations, an amount of work remaining is randomly selected from the range provided and then iterations are run by randomly applying a throughput and growth rate, based again on the ranges provided.

As you can see, this isn't running a basic burn down. This is an actual simulation based on the numbers provided using actual data drawn from your project's history.

The 500 resulting completion dates are graphed on a distribution chart, allowing us to determine the probability of each potential completion date.

[38]Magennis, T. (n.d.). Throughput Forecaster. Retrieved February 23, 2018, from https://github.com/FocusedObjective/FocusedObjective.Resources/raw/master/Spreadsheets/Throughput Forecaster.xlsx

[39]Magennis, T. (n.d.). Calculating Work Split Rate - Ground-Speed vs Air-Speed. Retrieved March 28, 2018, from http://focusedobjective.com/calculating-work-split-rate/

# Average

So let's take our current scenario and let's see how we do using our forecaster. We'll start with the average velocity of 13, 0 split rate, and 108 points to complete.

### Forecast Completion Date

**1. Start Date**  1/1/19

**2. How many stories are remaining to be completed?**
(enter the range estimate of stories. Tip: start wide and narrow as certainty increases)

Low guess  108                Highest guess  108

**3. Stories are often split before and whilst being worked on. Estimate the split rate low and high bounds.**
(often the throughput in the backlog is pre-split, but captured throughput post-split. Adjust for this here)

Low guess  1.00               Highest guess  1.00

**4. Throughput. How many completed stories per week or sprint do you estimate low and high bounds?**

Throughput/velocity data or estimate is for  2 weeks        14 days
(choose a time interval that throughput of velocity is measured in weeks from the list in the orange cell above)

Use historical throughput data **OR** enter a low and high estimate below. Use:  Estimate

Low guess  13                 Highest guess  13

Forecast with Average

We can see from the results chart below, that all 500 simulations complete on the exact same date as our velocity math - 18 weeks from now. This makes sense as there is no variance in the numbers provided. Therefore the same backlog size is always chosen, the same throughput is applied to each iteration, and there is no growth or split rate.

This is consistent with standard velocity math. We take a single value for velocity and divide it into the amount of remaining work and we get a single value. This is, presumably, the number of iterations remaining, and from it, we can calculate the date the work will be done.

**Results**

| Likelihood | Duration in 2 weeks's | Date |
|---|---|---|
| 100% | 9 | 5/7/19 |
| 95% | 9 | 5/7/19 |
| 90% | 9 | 5/7/19 |
| 85% | 9 | 5/7/19 |
| 80% | 9 | 5/7/19 |
| 75% | 9 | 5/7/19 |
| 70% | 9 | 5/7/19 |
| 65% | 9 | 5/7/19 |
| 60% | 9 | 5/7/19 |
| 55% | 9 | 5/7/19 |
| 50% | 9 | 5/7/19 |
| 45% | 9 | 5/7/19 |
| 40% | 9 | 5/7/19 |
| 35% | 9 | 5/7/19 |
| 30% | 9 | 5/7/19 |
| 25% | 9 | 5/7/19 |
| 20% | 9 | 5/7/19 |
| 15% | 9 | 5/7/19 |
| 10% | 9 | 5/7/19 |
| 5% | 9 | 5/7/19 |
| 0% | 9 | 5/7/19 |

Almost certain

Somewhat certain

Less than coin-toss odds. But if you are game?

Average Forecast Results

But this just isn't realistic. And it certainly isn't representative of our real world experiences. Throughput / Velocity usually varies a bit from iteration to iteration. Things happen; people are out, stories get blocked, we stay late to get more work done...

# Range

So let's run it again, but this time, we will use our velocity range instead of the average.

**Forecast Completion Date**

| | |
|---|---|
| 1. Start Date | 1/1/19 |

2. How many stories are remaining to be completed?

| Low guess | 108 | Highest guess | 108 |
|---|---|---|---|

3. Stories are often split before and whilst being worked on. Estimate the split rate low and high bounds.

| Low guess | 1.00 | Highest guess | 1.00 |
|---|---|---|---|

4. Throughput. How many completed stories per week or sprint do you estimate low and high bounds?

| Throughput/velocity data or estimate is for | 2 weeks | 14 days |
|---|---|---|

Use historical throughput data **OR** enter a low and high estimate below. Use:   Estimate

| Low guess | 8 | Highest guess | 16 |
|---|---|---|---|

**Forecast with Range**

Using our prior three iterations, the velocity had a low of 8, and a high of 16. We adjust the historical throughput low to 8 and the high to 16. We'll stick with a 0 split rate for this run.

In this simulation, the forecaster will randomly choose a through-put value between the ranges of 8 and 16 for each iteration. This is likely a more representative simulation. You might be thinking, "But what if the team's throughput has been consistently 15 or 16 and the 8 is a unique outlier?"

Excellent question. Remember that we are currently contrasting this method to our standard way of forecasting; use the last iteration or an average of the last few. We've seen the average. Now we're looking at what happens when we use a range taken from recent history. We'll do another run with more historical data next.

For now, let's look at the results of the forecaster with the given range.

## Results

| Likelihood | Duration in 2 weeks's | Date | |
|---|---|---|---|
| 100% | 12 | 6/18/19 | |
| 95% | 11 | 6/4/19 | Almost certain |
| 90% | 10 | 5/21/19 | |
| 85% | 10 | 5/21/19 | |
| 80% | 10 | 5/21/19 | |
| 75% | 10 | 5/21/19 | |
| 70% | 10 | 5/21/19 | Somewhat certain |
| 65% | 10 | 5/21/19 | |
| 60% | 10 | 5/21/19 | |
| 55% | 10 | 5/21/19 | |
| 50% | 9 | 5/7/19 | |
| 45% | 9 | 5/7/19 | |
| 40% | 9 | 5/7/19 | |
| 35% | 9 | 5/7/19 | |
| 30% | 9 | 5/7/19 | |
| 25% | 9 | 5/7/19 | Less than coin-toss odds. But if you are game? |
| 20% | 9 | 5/7/19 | |
| 15% | 9 | 5/7/19 | |
| 10% | 9 | 5/7/19 | |
| 5% | 8 | 4/23/19 | |
| 0% | 8 | 4/23/19 | |

**Range Forecast Results**

This time, our 18 week projection is showing a 10 to 50% probability. 20 weeks has a 55 to 90% probability and 22 weeks and 24 weeks are 95% and 100% probable, respectively.

This confirms our already growing suspicion; the standard velocity burn down technique we've been using is often less reliable than a coin toss.

# History

Let's run it again, but this time, let's use some actual throughput history rather than an average or a range. To do this, we provide our throughput history for the past several iterations.

We then adjust the settings
to use data, rather than
an estimate. The forecaster
will now ignore the veloci-
ty/throughput range and use
the actual data we provided.

**Enter Samples Below**

| |
|---:|
| 16 |
| 8 |
| 12 |
| 8 |
| 15 |
| 9 |
| 10 |
| 15 |
| 16 |
| 8 |

Forecast Data

Rather than choosing a random number in a range, the
forecaster now selects a random throughput value from
our history. Using this technique, the forecaster is better
able to represent a true sce-
nario. If our throughput history is consistent with a few outliers,
the forecaster will run simulations that are consistent with a few
outliers. If our throughput history is highly variable, the forecaster
will run simulations that are highly variable.

**Forecast Completion Date**

**1. Start Date**                    1/1/19

**2. How many stories are remaining to be completed?**

Low guess — 108            Highest guess — 108

**3. Stories are often split before and whilst being worked on. Estimate the split rate low and high bounds.**

Low guess — 1.00          Highest guess — 1.00

**4. Throughput. How many completed stories per week or sprint do you estimate low and high bounds?**

Throughput/velocity data or estimate is for    2 weeks    14 days

Sample Data Stability

Use historical throughput data **OR** enter a low and high estimate below. Use:    Data    8%

< 10% Great, < 25% Good

**Forecast with Data**

You might notice that, this time, the settings have some additional
information in the lower, right-hand corner. This information gives
us an indication of our throughput stability. A variance over 25% is
less desirable. The higher the variance, the less reliable the forecast.

In this example, the variance of 8% is great.

## Results

| Likelihood | Duration in 2 weeks's | Date | |
|---|---|---|---|
| | 13 | 7/2/19 | |
| 95% | 11 | 6/4/19 | |
| 90% | 11 | 6/4/19 | Almost certain |
| 85% | 11 | 6/4/19 | |
| 80% | 11 | 6/4/19 | |
| 75% | 10 | 5/21/19 | |
| 70% | 10 | 5/21/19 | |
| 65% | 10 | 5/21/19 | Somewhat certain |
| 60% | 10 | 5/21/19 | |
| 55% | 10 | 5/21/19 | |
| 50% | 10 | 5/21/19 | |
| 45% | 10 | 5/21/19 | |
| 40% | 10 | 5/21/19 | |
| 35% | 9 | 5/7/19 | |
| 30% | 9 | 5/7/19 | |
| 25% | 9 | 5/7/19 | Less than coin-toss odds. But if you are game? |
| 20% | 9 | 5/7/19 | |
| 15% | 9 | 5/7/19 | |
| 10% | 9 | 5/7/19 | |
| 5% | 8 | 4/23/19 | |
| 0% | 8 | 4/23/19 | |

Forecast with Data

Using actual throughput history, our 18 week projection is showing a 10 to 35% probability. 20 weeks has a 40 to 75% probability. 22 weeks has a 80 to 95% probability and 26 weeks is 100% probable.

You will find varying outcomes, depending on your actual through-put history. It isn't always worse than the range. Sometimes it is better. Sometimes it's the same. But using the actual history always provides a more realistic simulation than using a range, so if you have the actual data, why not use it?

# Split Rate

Now, let's consider that the defined scope of this project has been growing. This is also natural. We've discovered new desirable features as we've gone along, and we've been progressively elaborating which naturally results in some expansion of the scope size.

We started with a population of stories that represented 34 work units. Looking at the work targeted, it has grown to 40 work units. That's a split rate (or growth) of just over 17.5%.

So, let's use 18% as an approximation for our split rate and run it one more time.

**Forecast Completion Date**

**1. Start Date**                                      1/1/19

**2. How many stories are remaining to be completed?**
[enter the range estimate of stories. Tip: start wide and narrow as certainty increases]

| Low guess | 108 | Highest guess | 108 |
|---|---|---|---|

**3. Stories are often split before and whilst being worked on. Estimate the split rate low and high bounds.**
[often the throughput in the backlog is pre-split, but captured throughput post-split. Adjust for this here]

| Low guess | 1.00 | Highest guess | 1.18 |
|---|---|---|---|

**4. Throughput. How many completed stories per week or sprint do you estimate low and high bounds?**

Throughput/velocity data or estimate is for        2 weeks              14 days
[choose a time interval that throughput of velocity is measured in weeks from the list in the orange cell above]

Use historical throughput data **OR** enter a low and high estimate below. Use:        Estimate

| Low guess | 8 | Highest guess | 16 |
|---|---|---|---|

**Forecast with Split Rate**

## Results

| Likelihood | Duration in 2 weeks's | Date |
|---|---|---|
| 100% | 13 | 7/2/19 |
| 95% | 12 | 6/18/19 |
| 90% | 11 | 6/4/19 |
| 85% | 11 | 6/4/19 |
| 80% | 11 | 6/4/19 |
| 75% | 11 | 6/4/19 |
| 70% | 11 | 6/4/19 |
| 65% | 11 | 6/4/19 |
| 60% | 11 | 6/4/19 |
| 55% | 10 | 5/21/19 |
| 50% | 10 | 5/21/19 |
| 45% | 10 | 5/21/19 |
| 40% | 10 | 5/21/19 |
| 35% | 10 | 5/21/19 |
| 30% | 10 | 5/21/19 |
| 25% | 10 | 5/21/19 |
| 20% | 10 | 5/21/19 |
| 15% | 10 | 5/21/19 |
| 10% | 9 | 5/7/19 |
| 5% | 9 | 5/7/19 |
| 0% | 8 | 4/23/19 |

Almost certain

Somewhat certain

Less than coin-toss odds. But if you are game?

Split Rate Forecast Results

This time, our split rate is 1.00 for the low, indicating no split, and 1.18 for the high, indicating that for every 50 units we start with, we end up with 59 units in final scope.

Now, our probability of completing in 18 weeks had dropped to a range of 5 to 10% and a much more likely completion is 24 weeks from now, with a 95% probability.

## Determining Split Rate

So far, we've hand waived over split rate. Now, let's dive into it a bit and see how we can determine a reasonable split rate range for our project.

A split is anything that causes a single item to become more than one item.

In some cases, this is an actual story split. In iteration planning, for example, we realize that we can actually split this story into smaller deliverable pieces.

In some organizations, this type of split has to follow a set of rules that indicate a story must always split into smaller stories that total the original estimate. In other organizations, a story may split into pieces that exceed the original estimate.

It is ultimately up to you to figure out how you want to handle this in your own place of work, but if you are asking my advice, split the story and estimate the work as it is now articulated. Don't worry about the original estimate/size. Forcing teams to stick to an original estimate when they discover a new way of executing on the work is an arbitrary rule that offers no additional value, and is practically guaranteed to result in more consternation and waste.

A second example of a "split" is an actual growth in scope. Say we deliver a feature and then learn that our customers want it enhanced in some way. This is essentially the same as a split. We had a single work item, which, when delivered, produced yet another work item.

Another possible example of a split is discovery of a defect. If you record defects in your throughput, then any time you discover a defect, it is essentially a split of the work item that generated the defect. You had one work item. You delivered it. You now have two work items related to the same customer value; the original work item, and the defect. In some organizations, throughput is based on delivery of value work. Defects don't count in these organizations. In others, all work is counted. I've waffled back and forth on this over the years and have pretty much landed in the, "it's up to you" camp. Whatever you do, do it consistently.

As we can see, split rate is a bit involved and may be hard to measure. I tend to start teams with a split rate of 1.5 to 2.0, indicating that for every one work item in the backlog, we will have

1.5 or 2.0 work items at completion. When introducing the concept, I'll ask a team to grab 10 items out of the backlog, take a look at them and give me ball park on how many work items will result from these 10; including or excluding defects in accord with their policy on defect sizing/tracking.

To measure actual split rate is a bit difficult, but not impossible. Let's say we are targeting to release a specific feature. Once a week or so, we record the total number of work items (or points) that need to be completed in order to deliver the feature, including the work already completed. Let's say that, at the beginning, we have 100 units to complete. By the time the feature is delivered, there are 175 units completed. We now know that the split rate is 1.75 - for every work unit we began with, we ended up with 1.75 work units.

It is important to measure the work completed. Otherwise, you may over estimate the split rate.

Say, for example, you discover 10 defects, but 9 of them are low priority and will not need to be addressed in this feature release. Then only one of those defects counts toward the split rate. Similarly, if you identify new work that doesn't get prioritized into the existing release (or may never get done), then it doesn't count in the split rate.

## Conclusion

Using this forecasting technique has provided some very tangible benefits.

The first is the improved accuracy of the forecasts. Using this technique, we get a much better understanding of the probability that we can hit a date. We get a better sense of when the work will be completed.

The second is the quality of the conversations as a result of using this technique. Teams are able to talks about probability and help make informed decisions about delivery. I've had numerous instances with this technique where, given dates and probabilities, we were able to move deadlines to a higher probability date. I've also had a few instances where we were able to clearly identify scope to reduce in order to meet an immovable date.

In the past, we believed that in order to be able to reliably forecast, we had to first stabilize our velocity. This was because we were using standard velocity math. Velocity math was hard to believe when we could *see* the data was highly variable. As it turns out, we should have generally been suspicious of velocity math.

Using the Monte Carlo Simulation technique, while a stable throughput is certainly beneficial, it is not necessary.

# Customer Metrics

So far, we've focused almost entirely in measurements that are about the team and process. But let's not forget, we're building software for a purpose. There is some end user in mind. Someone for whom we are building this software.

They have goals and objectives they are trying to achieve. Perhaps they want a great deal on their next retail purchase. Or maybe they're trying to organize an important event. Or possibly they're trying to monitor the health of a critically ill patient.

Whatever it is, they're looking to us to help them achieve their goals. It only makes sense that we take measurements that confirm we are, in fact, helping the customer achieve their desired end.

## Outcomes Over Outputs

I've worked with many companies who've conflated delivery of features with delivery of value. They begin with the assumption that a feature adds value to the customer. This is often the case, but it is not always so. Some features are rarely or never used, providing little to no realized value. Some features are used out of necessity, but actually detract from the customer experience, potentially offering negative realized value.

 Speed (output) is beneficial only if you are headed in the right direction (outcome).

Output measurements focus on quantity of delivery, such as the count of features delivered. As a result, output measures tell us how fast we are moving. Outcome measurements focus on quality of delivery - or more accurately, the impact of delivery, such as how many customers are engaging in a key activity. As a result, outcome measures tell us if we are headed in the right direction. Additionally, speed (output) is beneficial only if you are headed in the right direction (outcome).

## Know The Problem You Are Solving

I once worked with a client who became so obsessed with immediate revenue metrics that they would not allow themselves to innovate in certain areas. Essentially, the only measure that mattered for a new feature was whether or not it had a net positive impact on revenue. Revenue was their standard outcome measurement. This was, of course, measured in real time. If they tried three different button colors on the checkout screen, they'd go with the one that achieved a statistically significant higher rate of purchase. Easy enough.

But when they wanted to get into personalization features, the first thing they needed to do was learn more about the customer and their preferences. No matter what they did, an interface that gathered personal data about a customer also resulted in lower purchase rates than the control which gathered no personal data. As a result, no matter how much data a customer volunteered, no matter how much time and energy they spent on customizing their own profile, the experiment was ultimately killed because it generated fewer immediate dollars than the control. As a second order result, the company struggled to figure out personalization and fell behind competitors who were focused on providing a custom experience to each customer over the long term.

 Underlying every "requirement" is a problem to solve; a pain point that we hope to alleviate.

They were using measures that didn't align with their desired outcomes. They'd grown so accustomed to judging all features by the same criteria, they failed to think critically about the problem they were solving. While revenue generation can be, and often is a fine outcome, it isn't the only outcome. And in some cases, it is counter to the real goal.

Underlying every "requirement" is a problem to solve; a pain point that we hope to alleviate. Our goal should never be to build some functionality; produce some output. It should always be to solve a problem; realize an outcome.

I tend to use three questions to prompt thinking and help teams figure out the measurements that can help them determine if they've achieved the outcome.

## 1. What problem are you solving and for whom?

Here, we identify the key issue and the key person or persona. This is a business problem or a customer problem. This is not a solution.

"Display daily total of calories consumed at bottom of user food log," is an articulation of a solution.

"Users are having difficulty staying within recommended daily calorie ranges," is a better articulation of a problem.

From the former, we know we are done when the total is visible on the bottom of the page, whether or not users see this as valuable or helpful. From the latter, we know we are done when the user is more often staying within calorie ranges, which we believe is solving a problem they currently face.

If asking, "What problem are we solving?", doesn't lead to a good answer, then a simple 5 why approach[40] may help you get from implementation request to problem definition. Starting with the implementation request, "Display daily total of calories consumed

---

[40]Serrat, and Olivier D. "The Five Whys Technique." Asian Development Bank. November 15, 2017. Accessed Jan 18, 2019. https://www.adb.org/publications/five-whys-technique.

at bottom of user food log," ask "Why do our users need that?" For each answer given, ask again, "Why?", until you get to a root problem or need.

### 2. What stories would we hear upon success?

Let's assume we are successful in our efforts. Users are now better able to stay within their daily calorie ranges (and they are happy about it). What stories would we hear? What positive things would users say about this change?

Consider the situation from the perspective of your users. Would they be delighted that you put data on the screen? Maybe not. Would they be excited about staying within their daily calorie ranges? Maybe. Would they be energized over the reduction in weight? Probably so.

So what stories would they tell? What would they rave about? What positive things would they say?

### 3. How could you substantiate their stories?

How could you objectively confirm the happy stories your users might share? What measures would you need to prove the stories are factually accurate?

Knowing the actual problem you are solving helps you think clearly about the data you should track to help you assess whether or not you've actually solved the problem.

# Feature Use

It seems that one of the hardest things for a software company to do is kill a feature. We conceived of it, designed it, planned it, created it, tested it, and released it. How could we possibly kill it?

Yet, there are so many pieces of software out there awash with nearly useless features that the majority of users will never utilize.

There is a difference between a product that is loaded with features and a product that is bloated with features. That difference, as it turns out, is not determined by the creator, but by the consumer. If they don't use it, it is useless.

The impact goes beyond simply whether or not a feature gets used. The more features a piece of software has, the greater the learning curve and the more cognitive load required to use it. Software with more features is almost always harder to use. And software with more features is therefor harder to adopt in the first place. The more features you add, the more likely your existing users are going to fall out of love with your solution, and the less likely new users will fall in love in the first place. Jared Spool refers to this phenomenon as Experience Rot[41].

To avoid experience rot, we need to be judicious about the features we launch and the features we keep. There is plenty of material out there on product management and feature selection. Here, we'll briefly discuss feature retention and refinement.

There are a number of tools available on the market today for adding telemetry to your applications. These tools enable you to add small pieces of code to your software which then gather anonymous information about users and how they interact with the software. Using such tools, you can monitor a number of aspects of the software[42], including adoption rate[43], retention rate[44], and task

[41]"Experience Rot." UX Articles by UIE. August 10, 2018. Accessed October 18, 2018. https://articles.uie.com/experience_rot/.

[42]"Product Analytics - How to Measure Your Software Development Success." Towards Data Science. February 01, 2018. Accessed May 27, 2018. https://towardsdatascience.com/product-analytics-how-to-measure-your-software-development-success-7a6bc765dbab.

[43]Kenton, Will. "Rate of Adoption." Investopedia. March 12, 2019. Accessed April 19, 2019. https://www.investopedia.com/terms/r/rate-of-adoption.asp.

[44]"How to Calculate Customer Retention." Evergage. October 18, 2018. Accessed January 6, 2019. https://www.evergage.com/blog/how-calculate-customer-retention/.

success[45] to help determine if a feature is worth keeping around in its current form.

# Adoption Rate

Adoption rate tells us that people are using the new feature. Adoption rate might be how many users are upgrading to the latest release, how many users are subscribing to the new feature or service, or simply how many users are utilizing the new functionality.

Look at user adoption rate as a percentage of all users as opposed to as an isolated number. You may see an increase in the number of users for a new feature and think it is a success. However, it might turn out that the rate of adoption for the overall application is out-pacing the feature. In such a case, while feature adoption is growing, the percent of users interested in the feature may be in decline.

A basic adoption rate is the number of users who first use our feature in a given time period (F), divided by the days in the time period (D).

Adoption Rate = F/D

Let's take an example where for a given week (D=7), the number of customers who first use our feature (F) is 32. Our feature adoption rate (FR) is 32 users / 7 days or 4.57 users per day.

Let's now assume that during that same week, application grew by 57 users. This is the number of users at the end of the week less the number of users at the start of the week. This is different than the number of new users as other users may have stopped using the application as well. So this is the application growth (G) rather than adoption. The application growth rate (GR) is 57 users / 7 days or 8.14 users per day.

---

[45]"What Is A Good Task-Completion Rate?" MeasuringU. Accessed January 19, 2019. https://measuringu.com/task-completion/.

If we subtract GR from FR, we get a relative feature adoption rate (RF) of -3.57. While the feature is being adopted, it is happening at a rate slower than the overall growth of the application. This feature may not appeal to the majority of the users.

Let's assume instead, that the number of overall users only grew by 21. With G = 21, our relative feature adoption rate is now 1.57. The feature is being adopted at a rate greater than the growth of the application population. This feature is more likely to become commonly used.

Watch how this trends over time. A single measure is not very informative. On any given week there can be noise in the system. Maybe there was a big push for new subscribers causing a negative relative feature adoption rate and other weeks were all positive. Maybe the feature is more valuable to users at certain times of the monthly or annual cycle.

Adoption is interesting and important, but we also want to ensure people continue to use the new feature. This will help us understand if they find it valuable rather than novel.

## Retention Rate

Retention rate tells us that people are continuing to use the new feature. This is more important than adoption rate. Adoption may be about newness or novelty. People might start using a feature because it looks promising. Retention tells us more about whether or not they find it valuable enough to use more than a couple of times.

There are a number of ways to calculate retention rate. Among them are Retention by Day, Range Retention, and Rolling Retention. Retention by day is very granular and is sensitive to noise in the system, but can provide feedback on a daily basis when a feature first launches. Range retention smoothes out the noise, can be run for short or extended ranges, and is good for looking at patterns, but it obfuscates some of the details and requires you to have sufficient data (at least a full range). Rolling retention is good for looking at overall stickiness of an app and is very easy to calculate, but treats high activity and low activity users the same.

We are going to focus on range retention as it is the most applicable.

### Calculating Range Retention

To calculate range retention, you need three pieces of data:

1. Number of customers using the feature at the start of a period (S)
2. Number of customers who first used the feature during the period (F)
3. Number of customers using the feature at the end of the period (E)

Customer Retention Rate (CRR) = ((E-F)/S)*100

Let's say we are calculating retention for a 4 week cycle. If the number of customers using the feature on day 0 is 203, the number of first-time users between day 0 and day 28 is 55, and the number of customers using the feature on day 28 is 216, then our retention rate is:

((216-55)/203) * 100 = 79.3

If the retention rate for a feature is consistently low, then it may be time to consider sunsetting the feature.

# Task Success

There are a number of possible measures for Task Success, including completion rate, task time, and task level satisfaction.

Completion rate is a means of measuring how many users completed an intended activity. This gives us some indication of whether or not users are getting the intended value from the feature.

Task time is the amount of time it takes to complete an activity. This give us some indication of the investment a user needs to make, and may tell us that a particular task/process is too difficult.

Task level satisfaction tells us how a user feels about the task itself. This is usually measured via micro-surveys at the end of a task.

While time and satisfaction are valuable pieces of data, we are going to focus on the measure of binary completion rate. This is easy to measure, regardless of audience size, can be measured before software is even written via prototypes, and is considered a fundamental metric for products.

For binary completion rate, you define a scenario for a user to complete - such as scheduling an event, making a purchase, or inviting a friend. You monitor the number of users who began the task as well as the number of users who completed the task. There is no partial credit. Either they finished the task or they did not.

The completion rate is simply the number of users who finished the task divided by the number of users who started the task. If 10 users started and 9 users finished, your completion rate is 90%.

A completion rate of 100% is phenomenal. On average, completion rates are closer to 70% to 80%, depending on the actual task and context. No matter how well you design a feature, you can expect some small percentage of users who do not complete a task.

With these three measures, adoption rate, retention rate, and task success, we know if we are attracting users at a desirable rate, if they are returning, and if they are getting done what we hoped they'd get done.

# Looking for Correlations

While a balanced set of regular metrics is certainly valuable and advisable, there may be occasions when you want to measure additional items. Or there may reasons to take a deeper look at how your metrics relate to one another. Are there correlations in the data? Does pairing regularly correlate to code quality in any way? Does code coverage correlate to complexity?

Let me give you a concrete example where knowing about correlations might be desirable. Say you are on a team that has a history of not testing in order to improve their speed to delivery. The premise, of course, is that skipping tests means less work. And less work, means faster delivery. Without any actual data aside from anecdote, this proclamation seems logical.

But what if you had the data? What if you could measure velocity by coverage and prove that not testing means getting the work done faster?

To do this, you'd need to measure test coverage and velocity, and see if there's any correlation by plotting them on a scatter diagram.

## Scatter Diagrams

Let's start with a simple scatter diagram as an example. The following scatter diagram shows automobile prices by age of the vehicle.

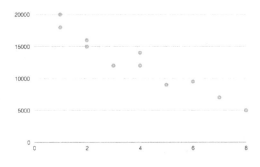

**Auto Price by Age**

Taking a quick look at this chart, you can probably see there is a natural trend line moving down and to the right.

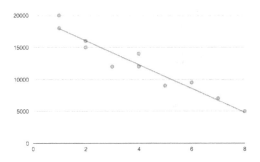

**Auto Price by Age with Trend Line**

This represents a negative correlation. A negative correlation is where as one value increases, the other value decreases. Alternatively, a positive correlation would trend up and to the right, showing that as one value increases, so does the other. If there is no correlation, there is no natural trend line.

## Velocity by Test Coverage

I've actually done this in a couple of environments, and the findings were the same each time. The team was insistent that not testing allowed them to move faster, because they could get more done in less time. They were typing less, so they were moving faster.

We decided to run an experiment for a period of time. We'd agree that certain functionality was to be tested and other functionality was not. Let's say this is an accounting system with Payables, Receivables, General Ledger, and Reporting. We agreed that Payables and Receivables should have tests and General Ledger and Reporting should not. You get the general idea.

We then looked at velocity (actually cycle time) for stories that had tests and those that did not.

Here's what we found:

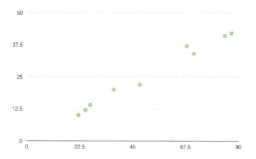

**Velocity by Code Coverage**

As we can see, this shows a positive correlation. That's right, the greater the test coverage, the higher the velocity. This is exactly the opposite of the team's original premise. At the very beginning of a project, not testing does allow for more rapid delivery. But in very short order, measured in days or weeks, certainly not months of effort, not testing catches up to you. Changes break things, and you have to go hunting down the source of the issue. You fix the issue and off you go. Two days later, some other area of the code is broken and you can't figure out why. It turns out a change your teammate made over a week ago broke this area of the code. Your teammate didn't know there was a dependency, so she didn't test this module.

This happens all the time. Mystery bugs. Difficulty finding the root cause. Not knowing you broke something.

These are all solved, or at least improved, by having tests.

Not to mention that tests actually help to ensure the code is better composed.

But, this section isn't about tests or test coverage, it is about data and correlations helping you to make informed decisions.

Here's a couple other scatter diagrams I've seen at client locations. They might surprise you.

## Velocity by Complexity

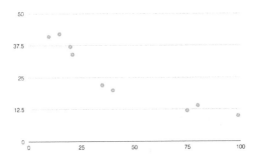

Velocity by Complexity

In this case we see a negative correlation between velocity and complexity. The more complex the code, as measured by cyclomatic complexity, the lower the velocity.

# Lead Time by Story Size

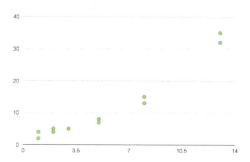

Lead Time by Story Size

Finally, we see a positive correlation between story size and lead time. In other words, the larger the story, the longer it took to deliver that story. This is logical. Bigger stories take longer.

But there was something interesting that we discovered in this particular experiment.

A 13 point story usually decomposed into some 3 and 2 point stories. Let's say we decomposed a 13 point story into four 3-point and two 2-point. The points went from a single story of 13 to 6 stories with a total of 16 points. A 13 point story required 33.5 days on average. A 3 point story required 5 days on average. And a 2 point story required 4.5 days on average. So even though we had more points, the stories took less time to deliver. The 16 points comprised of 2 and 3 point stories took an average of 29 days. The 13 point story took an average of 33.5 days.

The team could definitively see that when breaking stories down, it was okay that the points didn't add up to the estimate of the larger story AND that by breaking stories down, the team was able to deliver in less time. Not to mention, the options the team expanded through good story decomposition.

# Conclusion

I encourage you to look at correlations between the data points you have. Is there a correlation between velocity and value? Between coverage and cycle time? Between number of developers who touched the code and escaped defects? Team size and lead time? Number of hours colocated in the office and velocity?

I don't know what you're going to find, but I do know that what you find can help you make informed decisions for your teams in your context.

# Balanced Metrics

 Measure what you want to go up, but also measure what you don't want to go down.[46]

We've discussed a number of possible metrics to augment or even replace velocity. Rather than looking for the one true measure, it is important that we create a portfolio of measures that properly inform us about our process and progress. My advice to teams is to measure many things. Or, in the words of David J. Bland, "Measure what you want to go up, but also measure what you don't want to go down."

We know that measuring and making the measurement known changes behavior and thereby the outcomes. We know this from Hawthorne Effect. So even if we don't set targets, which would invoke Goodhart's Law, we still have a challenge in that measuring lead time might result in lower lead times, but we might sacrifice quality to do so. What are we to do?

Maybe we could measure many things. What if we anticipated that measuring lead time would possibly lead to lower code quality? The team moves faster by compromising on discipline. Well, we'd measure code quality, of course.

And what if we thought that maybe measuring quality and lead time would result in delivery of less value where the stories move quickly and are defect free, but don't meet customer needs? Then why not also measure feature use, revenue generated, or customer satisfaction?

---

[46]Bland, David J. "Measure What You Want to Go up, but Also Measure What You Don't Want to Go down." Twitter. Twitter, April 24, 2017. https://twitter.com/davidjbland/status/856643503606030336.

We've covered a number of metrics in this book, but our list is by no means comprehensive. Think about the system you are in and the standards you want to adhere to. How would you objectively know you are meeting those goals? How would you know if you are trending in the right direction in pursuit of those goals? Establish a set of measures you can take that inform you, and pay attention to them.

If you find a specific measure is not particularly informative or useful in pursuit of your goals, stop measuring it. As an example, at one client, we stopped performing customer surveys and focused on measuring interactions and conversions. Interestingly enough, we found it was relatively common for customers to give changes a low rating while simultaneously increasing their interactions and conversions. Our goal was conversions - enticing customers to take certain actions that lead to revenue for us. I'm not saying we didn't want customers to be happy with our software. What I am saying is customers often reported mediocre opinions of a change while simultaneously engaging more with the software in an increased revenue-positive way. In surveys, customers said they were neutral or even negative about a change, yet they increased their engagement, used the solution more, and generated more revenue for the company. The data from actual usage was more accurate than the opinions of the customers who took the time to complete the surveys.

This won't always be the case. I'm not advocating that companies don't survey customers. I'm advocating that you consider what you are trying to achieve and determine which measurements best inform you toward that end.

# A Starting Point

I am often asked what metrics a team (or teams) should use. This question often comes devoid of much detail, such as the make up of the team, how long they've been together, what pain they are experiencing, or what objectives they're trying to measure for. In these cases, I tend to advise teams to start with five basic metrics - feature use, lead time, cumulative flow, code quality, and team joy. These five metrics allow a team to determine if the customer is using the software, see if their time to delivery is improving, identify bottlenecks, know if they are managing consistent or improving quality, and learn if the team feels good about the work. With this information, they can tweak their efforts and find that sweet spot where they are moving as fast as possible without sacrificing quality and not burning out the team, all while adding value for the customer.

I am not saying these are the only measures you should use. I am not saying these measures are mandatory. What I am saying is, when I'm asked where a team should start without sufficient context or experience, this is where I tell them to start. It is a short, decent set of metrics that will inform them.

From there, they can adjust.

# Acknowledgements

I've had the great fortune of working with amazing people my entire career. There is no possible way I can acknowledge all who've had an impact on me and made this possible. So many have touched my life in so many ways. Herein I will attempt to acknowledge those who've altered my course significantly, or had a direct impact on the making of this book. Know that if I haven't mentioned you, you are in my heart and I am sorry for the oversight.

I love you all. Sincerely.

I started my career at a Law Firm in Cleveland Ohio where *Richard Kucia* and *Joe Sladick* mentored me as I moved from hobbyist to professional. Joe was especially influential as it was he who showed me the benefits of working in small chunks.

I soon started my own consultancy where I eventually partnered with *Brian Goleno* and *Mike Farona*, both of whom were influential in my continued growth. It was there that we first started experimenting with alternative approaches to software, and it was Brian who pointed me toward XP and then ThoughtWorks, a company I followed for years before joining.

At ThoughtWorks, I found a home, albeit temporary. The number of people with whom I had the opportunity to have great discussions and debate and to learn from is too significant to count. My time with ThoughtWorks was relatively short, but the impact was immense. My life changed for the better the day I became a ThoughtWorker.

Among all of the wonderful folks I worked with at ThoughtWorks, I especially want to acknowledge *Martin Fowler*. Martin has not only made great contributions to the software community as a whole, but for me personally. On more than on occasion, Martin took time out to have a one on one conversation with me. In each instance, he shared valuable insights and advanced my thinking.

Through the ThoughtWorks network, I had the opportunity to meet and interact with *Jeff Patton, Dan North*, and *Dave Hoover*. All three have influenced and helped to shape my thinking around teams, metrics, and the craft of making software.

In leaving ThoughtWorks, I joined LeanDog as a partner. There I had opportunity to work with *Jeff Morgan* who is one of the most passionate developers I know. Jeff and I would have long discussions on all things software over a beer or two. His perspective was invaluable and often pushed me to reevaluate my own perspective.

*Matt Barcomb* eventually joined us at LeanDog. He and I never got the opportunity to work on a project together, but we did have opportunity to talk philosophy and approach. Matt's sarcastic whit is bested only by his deep insights. Little did he know it, but one snark from him often lead to days of research for me.

As my exposure to the agile community grew, I had the fortune to meet and spend quality time with many of its founders and leaders. What I thought I knew was challenged and I turned from being the "expert" to being a beginner, which I've tried to be ever since. Related specifically to the material in this book, I recall conversations with *Diana Larsen, Ron Jeffries*, and *Jon Kern* as especially influential.

At Groupon, I had a unique opportunity to take everything I'd learned and put it into practice. My small team started a movement within Groupon Engineering to put people above process, and to foster Autonomy, Connection, Excellence, and Diversity. These are the cornerstones of OnBelay's philosophy and mission today.

When I started out to write a book, I struggled. I couldn't figure out how to start. I wasn't sure anyone wanted to hear what I had to say. I was afraid of putting in long hours for zero reward. *Johanna Rothman* took time out of her busy schedule to have a frank and very helpful talk with me. Were it not for Johanna, this book would most certainly not have happened.

Of course, none of my journey was possible without the continued support of my family. *Terri and Ladd Puskus, Richard and Marilyn Norton, Rick Norton, Jennifer Troutvine, Courtney Norton,* and *Sean Norton* made up my greatest support network and gave me purpose in life.

And in this past year, as I wrote this book, nobody has been more influential and supportive than my partner in business and in life, *Diane Zajac.* She's given me the time and space to write, encouraged me (even pushed me) to keep going, been there to bounce ideas off of, shared her own insights, and worked hard to help me edit the text into something people might actually enjoy reading.

In writing this section, I've looked back on my career and I see the faces of hundreds of friends smiling back at me.

I am truly fortunate.